OUR COMPETITION

is the World

by

Stan Baker

First Edition: 2012

© 2012 Stan Baker. All rights reserved.

© Lulu Publishing

Editor: Victoria Baker

Cover Artwork and Design: Stan Baker

Photography: Stan Baker, Wikimedia Commons, Enrique Arévalo, Fotolia, and ISI Photos

Artwork: Stan Baker and Allan Ledesma

Graphic Design and Layout: Stan Baker

Back Cover Photograph (ISI Photos): Rubio Rubin of the United States U-17 National Team after a 3-1 win over Brazil - December 4th 2011.

Title: "Our Competition is the World." – Claudio Reyna

ISBN: 978-1-300-04165-8

APPRECIATION

☺ To my wife Rocío and son Santi, who have always supported me along the way, and who have never doubted my dreams.

☺ I would also like to thank my friend, colleague, graphic artist and coach, Allan Ledesma, for his help in creating graphics for this book.

PROLOGUE

I am pleased to have the opportunity to help my friend Stan Baker in his request to add a few words in the prologue of his new book. I remember meeting Stan for the first time at a Region IV camp at Linfield College outside of Portland, Oregon in the summer of 2007. I was serving at the time as a Region IV staff coach and was partnered with Stan's Oregon 94 Boys team. I have had regular contact with Stan and have seen a number of his teams compete up through the 2010 version of the Region IV Camp.

There was no doubt that the Oregon players held a deep respect for their coach, and this was evident both on and off the field. It was clear from the beginning that Stan's main goal was the betterment of his players first as human beings and second as soccer players. He always acted with class and was a positive role model. Each year he brought in a group of players that reflected the diverse nature of the Portland soccer community that made up the majority of his teams.

The passion he holds for the game is contagious, and this was evident in the type of play that I observed from his players. Stan's teams have continually displayed an attractive style of possession based attacking soccer. Various players from his teams, including present U-17 National Team member, Rubio Rubin, have been called into the residency program in Bradenton. I believe that there are many fine coaches at the youth level in the United States, and Stan is one of them.

He is knowledgeable, organized, a good listener, professional and an inspirational teacher of the game.

Stan, I wish you well in your book and in your future endeavors.

Michael Ndoumbe
United States Soccer Youth National Team Scout, Region IV Head Coach, MLS Match Evaluator, and former Cameroun International.

For the group of instructors at ATFA (Asociación de Técnicos de Fútbol Argentino/Argentine Soccer Coaches Association), we saw Stan's taking on the two year ATFA Course (Pro and Youth Licenses) as a wonderful challenge. Here was someone coming from a country where soccer is not the most popular sport, and that up to this point has not had a huge impact on the world game; nevertheless, our expectations were high as we prepared to meet him.

We wondered, what he knew, how much he might feel the passion for our most popular sport, how he would handle the various training sessions and other questions asked of him. Although his command of Spanish is near native, it is always a challenge to take a course such as ours in one's second language.

Honestly it has been for me and the coaching staff at ATFA a hugely positive surprise. He knew everything, a lot of theory, he had a solid disposition for running training sessions, an ease in dealing with his players, good vocal control, warmth and a great joy and passion for the sport. It is an honor for us that he is writing a book, certainly something we have left with him over two long years of studies and a full week of rigorous tests, trying to achieve excellence in various concepts of the game.

Stan, you've achieved it, you are and will be a great coach. And a great honor for us.

Congratulations!

Enrique Borrelli
ATFA (Asociación de Técnicos de Fútbol Argentino/Argentine Soccer Coaches Association) Instructor, Youth Coordinator at Club Atlético Independiente, and former professional at Club Atlético River Plate.

I considered it an honor when my good friend Stan Baker asked that I write some words for his book. During my time as an author and a coach, I have met many people involved in our beautiful game; Stan is one of the most passionate I have known. The first time I met him was at the inaugural FIFA recognized coaching course run by the Escola Brasileira de Futebol at the CBF in Brazil.Over the duration of the CBF course, it was clear that Stan had a deep understanding of the philosophy and the history of the South American game. In the classroom I observed his profound knowledge of theory, and on the field I witnessed his natural ability to run training sessions. Having been a classroom teacher for so many years, he has developed a very good command with his voice, is organized and communicates clearly to the players. I feel that what he learned in Brazil will make his training sessions an even richer and more enjoyable experience for his players in the United States.

Stan and I maintain ongoing communication regarding player development, and I have no doubt that what motivates him is his desire that children in the United States fall in love with the game of soccer, just as he fell in love with the magic of Brazil - 1982, he is clearly a devotee to the beautiful game.

Stan, I would like to take a moment and wish you the best with your book and your future influence on the game in the United States.

Eduardo Andriatti Paulo
Brazilian CBF/FIFA "A" License coach and author of Brazilian Training Games, Brazilian Soccer Academy - Volumes I and II and Coaching Creativity Through Small Sided Games

🌐 A Brazilian National Team for Subbuteo Table Soccer.[1]

---

[1] Photograph: Released to public domain by Sportingn - Wikimedia Commons 2008.

INDEX

LEGEND

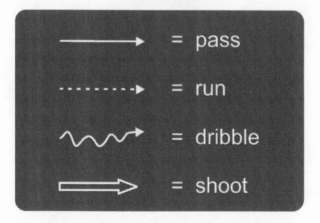

(These are the symbols for the graphics that appear throughout this book.)

"If you do what you have always done,

you will never get farther than you

have always gotten."

Horst Wein

INTRODUCTION

"It is the supreme art of the teacher to awaken joy in creativity and knowledge." – Albert Einstein

In writing this book, my aim is to provide coaches who work with all levels of youth soccer players, a resource to support the implementation of the recently developed United States Soccer Curriculum. (* see http://www.ussoccer.com/Coaches/Coaching-Education/Coaching-Home.aspx) The curriculum, developed in part through the research and personal experience of United States Boys Technical Director Claudio Reyna, and written by Spanish coach Javier Perez, was unveiled at the player development summit at the Nike campus in Beaverton, Oregon in April of 2011. Much time and thought was put into this document with the idea that it act as a roadmap for the improvement and the development of players in the organized player base in the United States. The curriculum's four main areas of focus include   the importance of <u>development over winning</u>, <u>quality training sessions</u>, <u>appropriately complex training sessions</u>, and the nurturing of a <u>fun and inspiring environment</u> for all players.

It is important to clarify that this book is not intended to take the place of the new curriculum, but rather to act as a supplement to help with its implementation. The ideas found in this book are certainly not the only way to approach player development. They are ideas that I have acquired from my own coaching experience, as well as through observing and listening to highly respected and knowledgeable coaches from here in United States and around the world. It is also not my intention to imply that we should copy everything that other countries are doing. I believe that we should be aware of what is working for the top soccer nations and to take that which can help us improve the development of players here in the United States. We should also be open to new ways of thinking about player development.

No doubt there is a tremendous amount of information available to coaches these days in the form of books, videos, and the Internet etc..., but only a fraction of this information is truly useful and of high quality. I have spent years sifting through a large quantity of information in order to put into these pages the most valuable and helpful material that I have found regarding the development of youth soccer.

The book's scope includes the formative stage of player development from ages 7-14, with the majority of the emphasis on the 11-14 age level which is considered the golden age of learning. It is organized around the four main pillars of the newly developed curriculum. The book is not meant to be a manual for 11v11 tactics, nor is it meant to be a manual for teaching correct technique. I do, however, provide some graphics in order to explain concepts related to style of play. When providing examples in the 11v11 game, I use the 4-3-3 system which is recommended by the United States Soccer curriculum. Since many other books have been written about the aforementioned subjects, I will approach this topic from a slightly different angle.

I will begin by examining the importance of developing a coaching philosophy. Next, I will look at the differences between the two approaches to youth coaching: the win now approach and the long term development approach. I will explain how style of play correlates directly with the chosen approach to coaching, and I will look at the importance of communication with parents about coaching philosophy, development and style of play. I will explore the importance of understanding our players and providing them with a quality, appropriately complex, and enjoyable training program. Other topics of focus include creativity and skill development. Furthermore, I will provide ideas as to how to help create a deeper and broader soccer culture amongst our players. I will wrap up by focusing on areas that continue to pose challenges for the development of youth soccer in the United States and will look at some ideas proposed by prominent members of the United States soccer community as to how to work around these obstacles.

"Education is not the filling of a pail; it is the lighting of a fire."
- W.B. Yeats

Although it may not be openly apparent, youth coaches can have a huge impact on shaping the long term culture of United States soccer. Coaches have the power to kindle the passion our players have for the game and to nurture their creativity. They can encourage youngsters to follow world class soccer on television and set them on the path of romance with the ball. Our youth coaches can create an environment where our players are inspired to challenge themselves to their limits while also awakening them to the joy of the game. It is my hope that this book in some small way influences youth soccer coaches as they set out to inspire their players.

✯ The passion for the game: a group of priests playing in Madrid, Spain.[2]

---

[2] Photography: Ramón Masats – Seminaristas jugando fútbol (1959).

18

CHAPTER 1

Developing a Coaching Philosophy

"What is the plan you have? What is your style of play? What's your philosophy? What do you teach them? What do you do with your staff? If you don't address that, then what are you doing? Going from week-to-week trying to win games?" – Claudio Reyna (United States Soccer Technical Director)

Developing a coaching philosophy is similar to developing a roadmap for traveling. Just as there are no two roads that follow the exact same path, no two coaching philosophies will ever be exactly alike. Coaching philosophies may take various forms, with each helping to reach the same destination. The importance that a written philosophy of coaching plays in communicating a coach's plan to parents and players cannot be overstated. It is much more difficult to take a group where you want them to go without some direction. On the following pages you will find my coaching philosophy. I am focusing on this first in order to give a general idea of what I believe about the game, and how I approach coaching.

Here are a few things I try to remember before stepping on the field.

☑ 72% of participants quit youth sports in the United States before the age of 13.

☑ The top four reasons why they quit:

1. The coach doesn't understand me.
2. I don't play enough.
3. The practices aren't fun.
4. There is too much emphasis on winning.

☑ The number one reason a child comes to practice:

1. "TO PLAY"

☑ The <u>one</u> thing that a coach working with players ages 6-10 must teach the players is:

1. "TO LEARN TO LOVE TO PLAY SOCCER."

Karl Dewazien

(Coaching Director of California Youth Soccer Association – North)

🌐 Children must have time to play.[3]

---

[3] Artwork: A.N.E.P. – Consejo de Educación Primaria – Uruguay.

LONG TERM PLAYER DEVELOPMENT OVER A WIN NOW APPROACH

☑ "The outcome of our children is infinitely more important than the outcome of any game they will ever play."

Karl Dewazien (Coaching Director – California North)

☑ "We are forming young human beings and not just soccer players."

Horst Wein (Author and internationally renowned coaching mentor.)

☑ One of a coach's main goals should be to pass on to the players the passion and love he or she has for the game.

☑ We should teach the players to respect the laws of the game, their teammates, the referee, opponents and themselves.

☑ "Players should be encouraged to play a variety of positions early on with more specialization coming after U-14."

Mauricio Marques (EBF- Instructor for the Brazilian Federation)

☑ "Up to the teenage years, the emphasis should be the player, the player, the player."

Dr. Tom Fleck (Founder of the National Youth License)

☑ Up to age 13 it is best to teach important concepts rather than a lot of team tactics. For Example: Encourage players to move away with a change of speed after a pass, to support the ball by getting "into the light" (proper angle to receive a pass), to disguise one's intentions, etc...

☑ Speaking about La Masia in Barcelona - "Some youth academies worry about winning, we worry about education."

Xavi Hernandez (F.C. Barcelona and Spain)

☑ "At a young age, winning is not the most important thing. The important thing is to develop creative and skilled players with good confidence."

Arsene Wenger (Head coach at Arsenal)

☑ Coaches should encourage players to have a balanced view of winning and losing, with the definition of success based on each player's own effort, preparation, and personal improvement.

John Wooden (Former Head Basketball coach at UCLA)

☑ "When one knows how to play, there is no need to employ means that go against the spirit and the skill of the game."

Jose D'Amico (Former FIFA and Argentine Coaches Association – Instructor)

☑ "A youth coach who wins almost everything has not worked for the future of his players rather for his own self-interest."

Horst Wein (Author and internationally renowned coaching mentor.)

☑ The fact that a team wins at the youth level does not necessarily mean that the players are developing to their maximum potential. One must ask what style of soccer they are playing. How do they score their goals? Are they relying primarily on bigger, stronger players?
Do they tend to play kick and rush? Do they play the ball on the ground or lift it mostly in the air?

☑ A coach's definition of success must be partly based on how many players return to play the following year.

☑ "Parents are paying for development, not trophies. It's cheaper to buy a trophy with your name on it than pay the club fees."

Jacques Ladouceur (Former U.S. National Team Player)

QUALITY TRAINING: GAME ORIENTED, PROPER INTENSITY, FOCUS AND EFFORT

☑ "Good coaches use the basic criteria of street soccer for their vision of grassroots development; they realize that these elements produce a natural process that gives the most efficient training for young kids."

Rinus Michels (Former Dutch National Team Head Coach)

☑ "The ideal training session is that which reproduces the intensity and the emotions of competition."

Telê Santana (Former Brazilian National Team Head Coach)

☑ "Consequences are not considered punishments. Using consequences in practice will increase focus, intensity and competition."

Dr. Ron Quinn (Author, educator and former U.S. Youth Soccer National Staff Coach)

☑ "For maximum player development, it is important that youngsters are introduced to a competitive environment at the youth level where they are presented with minimal to moderate amounts of stress during practice sessions."

Laureano Ruiz (Former Head Coach and Youth Academy Coordinator at F.C. Barcelona)

☑ "Success is no accident. It is hard work. Perseverance, learning, studying, sacrifice and most of all love of what you are doing or learning to do."

Pelé (Three time World Champion with Brazil – player of the century)

APPROPRIATELY COMPLEX PROGRESSION: DEVELOPING GAME INTELLIGENCE, PERCEPTION, AND TECHNIQUE

Appropriate complexity, simplified games to 4 goals, rondos, futsal, problem solving, emulation, and repetition.

☑ "It is important to know the age level one is coaching and to not train the youngsters like adults. A coach should get to know the players on an individual basis and should demand from them what their physical, mental and technical abilities allow."

Horst Wein (Author and internationally renowned coaching mentor.)

☑ "Players should have plenty of space and time when they are at the beginning stages of their technical development. They should progressively have time and space taken away as they gain a better control of the ball. Allowing players the correct amount of time and space will allow them to develop better habits, to be more creative and to avoid being suffocated during the game."

Laureano Ruiz

☑ "Players in the beginning stages of development should not be asked to play one touch or to lift their heads and look around when dribbling. It is difficult enough for them as it is. They should first focus on gaining confidence with the ball."

Laureano Ruiz

☑ Youth Players should frequently work on the following items:

1. getting more comfortable controlling the ball

a. reception b. first touch c.) juggling d.) dribbling

2. 1v1 situations a.) getting past opponents b.) shielding the ball

3. proper passing, heading, and finishing techniques

4. perception and decision making in 2v1, 2v2, 3v2, and 3v3 situations

☑ "Soccer is a game that begins in the head, flows through the heart and ends in the feet."

Horst Wein (Author and internationally renowned coaching mentor.)

☑ "The fastest player is not the one who runs the fastest yet the one who solves the game's problems the fastest."

Cesar Luis Menotti (Head coach of World Champion Argentina - 78)

☑ "Simplified games should frequently be played to four small goals rather than to just two. This will help players improve their decision making and perception."

Horst Wein

☑ Youth soccer players benefit from playing futsal where the benefits include: touching the ball twelve times more than in soccer, the creation of countless 1v1 duels, the development of game intelligence through more simplified tactical situations, and emphasis on skill rather than on physical contact.

☑ "Coaches must make an effort to teach children problem solving leadership and critical-thinking skills as much as they teach them how to shoot a soccer ball."

Dr. Ron Dr. Quinn

☑ "The coaches job should be to guide the players to solving problems on their own. Players who discover things for themselves will have the lessons more deeply ingrained. For this reason, coaches should ask open ended questions at practices instead of providing all the answers. Questions should begin with words such as what, when or how. Examples: What is the advantage of changing the point of attack? How does my teammate tell me where he wants the ball?"

Horst Wein (Author and internationally renowned coaching mentor.)

☑ During matches the coach should allow players to make their own decisions. Constant yelling of instructions to players from the touchline will impede in their development and will only serve to distract them from being focused on the game. The coach should spend most of the time sitting on the bench, observing and taking notes which will serve to plan the next training session.

☑ Youth soccer players should learn how to play on a variety of surfaces including cement, futsal courts, artificial turf, grass, sand, dirt etc...

☑ Different size/texture balls such as tennis balls and Brazilian mini rubber balls should be used in youth development.

☑ Youth players should watch professional players as much as possible in person and also watch them on television/videos/You tube etc... This will allow them to learn and emulate the movements and tricks of the professionals.

☑ "If tennis, baseball, volleyball, and basketball are sports in which players use repetition to improve specific skills, why not use a wall with measurements of a goal, where each player can practice finishing 50 times a week, 200 times per month, 2,000 times in ten months until he or she becomes an expert finisher."

ATFA (Association of Argentine Football Coaches)

☺ A well-loved ball.[4]

"First is philosophy. The start of everything is you decide the style of play." – Real Madrid manager Jose Mourinho

---

[4] Photograph: Fotolia.

ENCOURAGING A POSSESSION ORIENTED ATTACKING STYLE OF PLAY

☑ "Soccer should always be played in an attacking style. It should be a show or spectacle."

Johan Cruijff (Former great for Ajax, Barcelona and Holland)

☑ "If you have the ball the opponent doesn't."

Johan Cruijff

☑ "Short and to feet."

Alfredo Di Stéfano (Former legend for Real Madrid, Argentina and Spain)

☑ "My only way to interpret the game is that the ball is played on the ground."

Marcelo Bielsa (Former National Team Coach of Argentina and Chile)

☑ "If God had wanted us to play football in the sky, he'd have put grass up there."

Brian Clough (Former Head Coach at Nottingham Forest)

☑ "A 0-0 scoreline is like a Sunday without sun."

Alfredo Di Stéfano

☑ "I pass and I move, I help you, I look for you, I stop, I raise my head, I look and, above all, I open up the pitch. The one who has the ball is the master of the game. That's the school of Joan Vilà, of Albert Benaiges, of Johan Cruijff, of Pep Guardiola."

Xavi Hernandez

☑ "When we lose possession everyone helps to win the ball back. When we gain possession, everyone who knows how joins in the attack."

Alfredo Di Stéfano

☑ "Whenever I put a team together my aim is to make it mobile and attack-minded."

Roberto Falcao (Former great for Sport Club Internacional, Roma, and Brazil)

☑ "I prefer to win 5-4 than 1-0."

Johan Cruijff

🌐 World Cup Brazil – 1950.[5]

---

[5] Artwork: Fotolia

NURTURING A LOVE FOR THE GAME

☑ "Coaches should provide a variety of games and activities in practice sessions. These may include non-soccer games such as tag games. This will allow for enjoyment and help maintain motivation."

Mauricio Marques (Brazilian CBF Instructor)

☑ "The game is the best teacher. The coach is really a substitute voice. We want the players to hear the silent voice, the game. The game is actually talking to you."

Manny Schellscheidt (Former Head Coach – U.S. Youth National Teams)

☑ Overcoaching hurts a player's enjoyment of the game. "I am grateful to my father for all the coaching that he did *not* give me."

Ferenc Puskas (All-time great player for Hungary and Real Madrid)

☑ "A player can only achieve his maximum when he is enjoying himself." - Johan Cruijff

☑ "We have to reconstruct a sensation, something very profound: let us go back to when we were 14 years old when we played against our neighborhood rivals and nothing else mattered than that, neither the place nor the time. Nothing - Because the only thing that interested us, precisely, was to play. "- Marcelo Bielsa

☑ "To play football one should not suffer. What is done while suffering cannot turn out well."

Carles Rexach (Former player for F.C. Barcelona and Spain)

☑ "Children learn by playing, on the condition that the game brings them joy." - Ramon Maddoni (Boca Juniors Youth Academy Coordinator)

🌎 A children's mural inside River Plate's Estadio Monumental - Buenos Aires, Argentina.

The author at the CBF training center – Teresópolis, Brazil.

CHAPTER 2

Winning Now vs Long Term Development

"At a young age, winning is not the most important thing. The important thing is to develop creative and skilled players with good confidence." – Arsene Wenger (Arsenal Head Coach)

Before starting out with a new coaching assignment, a youth soccer coach must decide whether to go down one of two paths. One of these paths leads to the win now model, and the other path leads to the player development model. Almost every decision that a coach makes throughout the season can be linked back to this choice. As professional youth academies take hold in the United States, this decision should be made automatically. In most other parts of the world where professional soccer organizations exist, the priority of the professional youth academy is already laid out; and that is to develop as many top flight players to play in the first team as possible. The focus early on in the development process is not on winning a specific league or tournament, but rather on how the players are playing and progressing. The best of these academies also care about educating and forming human beings. Barcelona is perhaps the best example of this where numerous first team players have been developed in their youth academy.

"With the overemphasis on winning in this country, we are creating a nation of kids who can win but cannot play the game." – Dr. Jay Martin (Coach, author, and former president of the NSCAA – National Soccer Coaches Association of America)

In order to allow our players in the United States to reach a higher level of development, it is essential that as many clubs, academies and teams, adopt this philosophy as possible. U.S. Soccer Development Director Jill Ellis states: "It is certainly time for us as a soccer community to acknowledge the coaches who inspire a love of the game, and to truly appreciate the coaches who develop our future national team players. It is time, perhaps, when getting one special player to the next level is recognized as more important than a 19-0 season." Some will argue that there is no need to choose one approach over the other, but this premise is false. It is essential to recognize that each of these models is separate and distinct with completely different goals and outcomes. In fact they inherently oppose each other. This becomes clear as one explores each of these models more in depth. With this said, if the development process is done properly, <u>winning becomes a by-product</u>.

CHARACTERISTICS OF THE WIN NOW MODEL ACCORDING TO HORST WEIN:

1. The tendency is to choose players who are more developed physically, especially the bigger and stronger ones. They are the starters. Less attention is paid to their technical ability, regular attendance, attitude, effort at practice, and their relationship with teammates.

2. There is less of a chance given to the younger, smaller players who have not yet developed physically. Soccer is antidemocratic.

3. Beginning at eight years old there is an overemphasis on team tactics.

4. Only one system of play is applied.

5. The long pass is given immediately after winning possession. The team is hurried and plays more quickly than it is able.

6. The team plays direct and tends to favor vertical play. The goalkeepers always punt the ball and take long goal kicks.

7. There is little intent on building the play. The ball goes frequently straight to the forwards bypassing the midfield via long passes.

8. When attacking, the team rarely switches the point of attack.

9. The person in charge is a coach who instructs with the goal of winning the game and the championship. The player must obey the coach who instructs from the touchline.

10. In search of victories, the coach instructs his players to push the limits of the laws of the game and to cheat the opponents and the referee. The ends justify the means.

11. The game is played AGAINST the ball. There is little time or space for fakes and creative moves.

12. There is premature specialization in one determined roll or position. The same players play most of the games while the substitutes play little.

13. Young players are exposed prematurely to the adult game. It takes years for the same habits to develop that adults show in the 11 v 11 game.

14. An excessive amount of time is dedicated to physical training because with these methods one can achieve greater results in a shorter amount of time.

15. The traditional methodology of coaching is prevalent in training sessions.

16. Sporting results are valued more than the person. Poor behavior is frequently overlooked in order to gain immediate results.

CHARACTERISTICS OF
THE LONG TERM DEVELOPMENT MODEL
ACCORDING TO HORST WEIN:

1. Everyone plays and not only the stronger players. During the selection process, preference is given to the more intelligent and skilled players.

2. Good behavior on and off the field is one of the criteria for selecting players.

3. Everyone has a right to play independent of their physical capacity. Soccer is democratic.

4. The game serves to evaluate ability level and to gain tactical experience.

5. The culture of possessing the ball is prevalent. The team's play is not rushed.

6. Everyone touches the ball. There are mostly shorter passes along with support for shorter passes. The goalkeeper tends to throw the ball out rather than punting.

7. The ball generally advances from the backline to the midfield and then to the forwards with play based on the principles of communication and cooperation.

8. With the objective of creating space for penetration, the point of attack is frequently changed.

9. The one in charge is a coach who stimulates learning with the goal of improving the play of his player and his team. The player carries out the following action in terms of what he has observed and decided on the field. The coach does not decide for him.

10. Sportsmanship is taught, honesty, respect for the laws of the game, and to be loyal to them when in confrontation with opponents.

11. The game is played WITH the ball, caressing it. Situations are provided where players are allowed to try out new fakes and to use fantasy and imagination.

12. Everyone receives various opportunities to experiment playing different positions during the competition. Everyone plays regardless of his skill level.

13. The competition is adapted in each phase to fit the development of the child and his physical and intellectual capacities.

14. Respect is given to the natural development of the child and conditional and coordinative abilities are improved through a wide variety of games.

15. To best help a player's development, the application of an active methodology should be prevalent.

16. Priority is given to human development through sport. Sport is used as a classroom to teach lessons about life.

"Let us say that you and I coach two teams with kids that are 10, 11, and 12 years old and all are about equally good. You try to teach them to play good football, a passing game and with tactical basics while I tell mine to only play long balls and try to shoot. I can assure you that [at first] I will always win against you, by using your mistakes. Intercept a bad pass and goal. If we however continue with the same training methods during a three year period, you will most likely win every game against us. Your players will have learned how to play while mine haven't. That's how easy it is." _ Laureano Ruiz (Former Head Coach and Youth Academy Coordinator _ F.C. Barcelona)

🌐 La Bombonera: Stadium of Boca Juniors - Buenos Aires, Argentina.[6]

6 Photograph: Helge Høifødt - Wikimedia Commons 2009.

✪ A player card for the great Alfredo Di Stéfano while a young player at River Plate in Argentina.[7]

(Alfredo Di Stéfano – above) The entire playing field fitted inside his shoes. From his feet the pitch sprouted and grew...He ran and reran the field from net to net. He would change flanks and change rhythm with the ball from a lazy trot to an unstoppable cyclone; without the ball he'd evade his marker to gain open space, seeking air whenever a play got choked off... He never stood still. Holding his head high, he could see the entire pitch and cross it at a gallop to prise open the defence and launch an attack. He was there at the beginning, during, and at the end of every scoring play, and he scored goals of all colours.– <u>Eduardo Galeano</u> (Uruguayan Writer)

---

[7] Photograph: copyright expired in Argentina - Wikimedia Commons 1940.

CHAPTER 3

Communicating the Long Term Development Philosophy to Parents and Players.

"When the whole world is running towards a cliff, he who is running in the opposite direction appears to have lost his mind." – C.S. Lewis (Irish author)

There is no doubt that the culture in the United States is one that measures success by winning. This culture of winning is deeply ingrained in our society and is evident in the hero status we give to coaches such as the American Football coach Vince Lombardi who is famous for proclaiming "winning isn't everything, it's the only thing." For this reason, those coaches who take up a definition of success that is anything different than winning, are going against the current of our society's culture. This brings about a challenge in itself and takes a coach with courage, conviction and the ability to put ego aside for what is best for the children. I would venture to say that the majority of coaches in the

United States understand that the long term development approach is what is best for players, but they either don't know how to go about implementing it, or external pressures from parents and club provide major obstacles.

Once a coach has chosen the long term development over the win now philosophy, it is extremely important to clearly explain to the parents and players of one's team the reasons for choosing such an approach. The first chance to do this is at the first team meeting of the year. Since most coaches don't hold the same credibility of someone such as the United States Soccer boys' technical director Claudio Reyna, who in the new curriculum calls for development over winning, it is essential that the coach prepare documentation that demonstrates that highly respected individuals around the world believe in such a philosophy. Parents should be made aware of the recommendations of the United States Soccer Curriculum during the meeting. This may be done by giving out a link to the United States Soccer website or by simply emailing the curriculum electronic file to the parents. As the curriculum is quite long it would not be appropriate to go over it in every detail. It would be better to allow parents time to look it over and then encourage them to come to you with any questions they might have.

It is also important to communicate to both the players and the parents what the team's definition of success looks like. So how does one go about doing this? First of all, the coach should prepare either a presentation handout or if possible, a Power Point slide presentation for the initial team meeting to help clarify the ideas behind the long term development philosophy. It is important to remember that this first meeting sets the tone for the coach's philosophy, but ongoing education is most definitely required. In fact it would be wise to hold a parent meeting once a month in order to maintain a level of communication regarding the importance of long term development, and the team's progress towards its objectives. This is especially the case if the team has never been taught the benefits of development over the win now approach in the past.

The first item to include in the initial presentation to the parents should be one's coaching philosophy. In the coaching philosophy, the coach should state that he is an enthusiastic proponent of long term development, and that he has evidence to back up his claims. After communicating the coaching philosophy, the coach should next point out the clear distinctions between the long term development and the win now approaches. Hopefully it is already clear how superior the long term development approach is when compared to the win now approach. If not, please read the earlier chapter that highlights the differences between the two approaches. In order to help give stability and backing to one's philosophy, the coach should point out that various credible sources also believe in the long term development approach. Here the coach may provide quotes, phrases and even photos of reputable soccer coaches and players who back the same philosophy. As many more parents are becoming familiar with the world game, it is quite reasonable to expect that the parents will know the names of big clubs such as Barcelona, Real Madrid, A.C. Milan, or Manchester United. In many cases at the elite clubs, players have been recruited by the club, or parents have sought out the elite club solely based on the clubs winning reputation.

For ongoing parent education coaches and clubs can use a website such as   www.korrio.com   where lines of communication can be set up with parents and players by posting articles, recommended books, pictures, videos, tactical situations, wall routine, juggling routine, a link to the United States Soccer curriculum etc... Here is a brief description of Korrio.

Korrio is a cloud-based service for organizing youth sports. Their focus is unifying and amplifying the sports life of every athlete. They provide every tool required to get a player on the field while providing an environment for staff, families and fans to share and build community. Korrio, founded in January 2009, plans to transform sports at every level for the 100+ million Americans who participate on teams.

korrio®

In order to further communication links with the parents and to help move the focus of success away from winning and onto specific areas of the game is to have engaged by taking stats during the games. This way they are engaged in the game, and they are not yelling instructions to the players.

I recommend creating a stats sheet where stat duty is assigned to various parents each game for monitoring. Buy a few of the small clipboards and you'll be ready to go. This will be a shared assignment so all parents get a chance to take part. The stats sheet may include things such as sequences of passes, the number of times that our team switched the point of attack, the number of times that we got to the end line, the number of 2v1 situations that we created etc… Shifting the focus from winning onto the various aspects of the game that you are trying to improve on will help redefine success. (*see the following page)

Without a doubt there will be some parents who identify themselves with the win-loss record of their child's team and don't completely buy into the long term development approach. In fact, some parents will never buy into long term development over the win now model. If these parents end up removing their child and transferring them to another club it will only be their child's loss. Hopefully the continued communication between coach and parents will help eliminate most of these situations. At the same time, it is important not to give in to parents who continually criticize the fact that the team is not winning every game. It is at this time when a coach's courage and resolve are tested that having a club coaching director who understands and supports long term development over the win now approach can help tremendously.

TEAM STATS

_____ VS _____

DATE: _____

1. PLAY OUT OF THE BACK SUCCESSFULLY TOTAL: _____

2. PLAY THROUGH THE LINES (backs to midfield) TOTAL: _____

3. SEQUENCES OF 7 PASSES OR MORE PASSES TOTAL: _____

4. CHANGE THE POINT OF ATTACK TOTAL: _____

5. CREATE 2V1 SITUATIONS TOTAL: _____

6. CROSS THE BALL FROM THE ENDLINE TOTAL: _____

7. CHANCES CREATED TOTAL: _____

8. GOALS SCORED TOTAL: _____

*Put each tally in the corresponding box, and then add them to get a total.

🌍 CBF Training Facilities in the quiet town of La Granja Comary outside of Rio de Janeiro. In the background is (Campo - 1) where the Brazilian Men's National Team trains in preparation for international tournaments.

CHAPTER 4

Questions to Guide Parents When Analyzing the Play of Their Child's Team

The ten questions found on the following pages are especially directed towards parents who have children 10 years old and above. Below this age level, the players are still very egotistical and focused on themselves rather than on any sort of collective play. The infamous swarm is actually just a reflection of the natural process. The best thing to do is to keep the numbers low for this age group since less players means more access to the ball and less suffocation by both teammates and opponents. This will ultimately lead to better player development. To avoid confusion and disappointment from parents, coaches of players under 10 years old should communicate to them that it is ok at this age level for the players to gravitate to the ball, and that the game played by the youngest players shouldn't reflect that of a professional team.

ANALYZING MY SON OR DAUGHTER'S TEAM — 10 QUESTIONS FOR PARENTS

1) Are the players attempting to pass the ball on the ground to teammates, or are most passes just played long and far into space?

2) Does the team try to possess the ball? How many passes does the average possession last?

3) Is the ball up in the air or out of play for a large part of the game?

4) Does the team pass the ball laterally from one side of the field to the other switching the point of attack? Are they patient in building an attack, or do they hurry to kick the ball forward?

5) How often is the ball passed backwards? On a more evolved team the ball should be played back once every three to four passes.

6) Does the team rely almost solely on kicking the ball forward to a big fast player up front to score, and on another big fast player in the back to cover for mistakes and send the ball forward? If so, what kind of soccer experience is the rest of the team getting?

(As the players move to a more advanced level of play we must remember that most defenders will be as big and fast as our team's primary goal scorer. Also, better players and well-organized teams learn to defend long straight passes quite easily.)

7) Does the game appear to be out of control? Are there frequent, consecutive changes in possession?

8) Are all players moving to create space or to support the ball, or does the team rely on only a few players?

9) Do the players always play in the same position on the field or is there a rotation?

10) Has the team evolved from the beginning to the end of the season? Has your child progressed as a player?

🌐 An Atlético de Madrid - Subbuteo table soccer team. [8]

---

[8] Photograph: GNU Free Documentation License - Wikimedia Commons 2011.

CHAPTER 5

A Better Understanding of Our Players

"The tragedy of coaching young players focuses on the fact that many coaches may know a lot about the game, but they don't know their young pupils." – Horst Wein

NICE TO MEET YOU

In order to better understand our players, the first thing we must do is to spend more time listening to them. At the beginning of each season, for example, a coach can show an interest in learning about his players by having them fill out a fun questionnaire focusing on their varying interests. This questionnaire can include soccer related items such as favorite player, team, soccer activity, personal soccer goals etc… and other non-soccer items such as favorite video game, type of music etc… Showing an immediate interest in each player will go a long way in gaining the trust and confidence of the group.

Since communication is crucial to maintaining team chemistry and in getting the most out of our players, it is beneficial to hold informal meetings once a month with each player. This is easiest done on free play days when there is no coaching involved in the practice session. During this time, the coach can pull individuals aside and talk to them about their progress and goals for the season. The coach who can make comments about the player's favorite team, player or even their favorite movie, will gain a deeper respect and trust from the players. It is important that these conversations be of a back and forth dialogue rather than a sermon. Of course if the time is not available at training sessions then phone calls and email can go a long way towards inspiring and gaining the confidence of the players. Sometimes sending a short email message mentioning something positive you saw from the player in practice can make a huge difference in their confidence.

"A coach must remember that he is a teacher and teachers also learn from listening to others. You must be more interested in finding the best way than having your way. Almost as much can be learned by listening to those under your supervision as from your peers and from those whose supervision you are under. We learn from listening, not speaking." _ John Wooden (Former Head Basketball Coach - UCLA)

Players and parents will appreciate this ongoing communication and in many cases the player will become more engaged in the practices and will respond in a positive manner. Team talks should mostly be in the form of a back and forth conversation where the coach listens to what the players are saying.

It is important to be conscious of the player's level of enthusiasm and body language. If they are truly engaged in the training session they will show it outwardly. When players are having fun and enjoying themselves, there is no need to transition away from a specific activity. Sometimes the group will be having so much fun that they can continue with the same activity for the entire practice. When the players lose track of time and express disbelief when they find out that practice is over, this is a sign that the practice went well. The coach should note which activities the players like best and repeat them more frequently.

AGE GROUP CHARACTERISTICS

"I always say to coaches, 'Know who it is you're coaching.' That's the most important thing. What's the age group? Know their characteristics. The personality of the age group. What excites them? Know the gender. Know the level they're playing in." – Bobby Howe (Former Director of Coaching Education at United States Soccer Federation)

5 to 8 years old

At this age children are starting to get more comfortable with their bodies, and they are exploring what they can and cannot do. They like to try out different types of movements such as running, jumping, spinning, rolling and throwing. They have a completely egocentric viewpoint of the world. Children at this age are still in the process of building the necessary experiences to interact with their surroundings and with others. During this period they like to use their imagination when playing. They lack empathy and the capacity to consider the thoughts and feelings of others. In order to help children build their own experience, the majority of the exercises should be focused on the individual (each player with a ball). The tactical component of the game should be based on small-sided games from 1v1 to 3v3 with no goalkeepers. Field size should be appropriate for the small-sided games and the ball should be a size 3. Practice sessions should be full of active play time with many breaks in between. <u>The most important thing a coach can do at this stage is create a safe environment in which the players are enjoying themselves while beginning to develop a love for the ball</u>. According to Sports Psychologist, Darren Treasure[9], children in this age group still make self-referenced rather than social norm referenced judgments of ability. They equate success with their own effort; therefore, they still believe that in order to improve their skills that they must practice more. Coaches of children at this stage must have patience, be organized, have a sense of humor, be very encouraging, and have a child's perspective on the world. No organized competitions should be played at this stage of development.

8 to 10 years old

This age is a very important period in the sports education of children, since for the vast majority of them it will be the first time that they take part in an organized sporting activity in which there is formal training and competition.

---

[9] <u>Motivation is More than a Question of Winning or Losing</u> – Darren Treasure Soccer Times, December 1998.

PSYCHO-PEDAGOGICAL CHARACTERISTICS:

At this age the players tend to abandon their egocentric attitude, and they begin to take the other players around them more seriously. Children of this age demonstrate a great disposition to play. They develop a more realistic attitude, while many of the infant myths disappear during this stage. They tend to have great respect for adult authority and the desire to learn from them. The ability to pay attention improves considerably during this period, and the child is able to participate in concrete activities for a considerable amount of time without being distracted. The children still relate success to effort and have an optimistic view of life.

PSYCHOMOTOR CHARACTERISTICS:

This is a period of balance with regards to the biometrical proportions. Growth is steady and without sudden changes. During this stage there is a considerable amount of neurological maturation along with high levels of muscular elasticity. Children of this age have the ability to maintain efforts with periods of self-regulation. There is a good level of overall coordination where the children can perform the vast majority of technical gestures that a sport such as soccer requires.

The players constantly seek out motor solutions for challenges posed by the games. They enjoy and demand almost constant activity.

10 to 12 years old

PSYCHO-PEDAGOGICAL CHARACTERISTICS:

During this period the players are capable of relating and associating concepts in time and space. They are interested in challenges in which they can measure their competitive level. It is the tendency of children of this age to move away from the world of childhood. At this age children begin to compare themselves more with others, and they begin to worry about the image they project to the world. Instead of relating success to effort as they have done previously, they begin to relate success to winning and losing. For this reason it is important that a coach guide the players towards a balanced approach to winning and losing. During this stage of development there is a noticeable increase in autonomy where the child can work alone without the constant support of an adult. The child begins to become aware of his possibilities and his motivations and consequently his behavior goes hand in hand with his personal perception. He is able to become an independent thinker.

PSYCHOMOTOR CHARACTERISTICS:

At this stage of the child's development, there is compensation between growth in length and in width along with a good relationship between weight and strength. For this reason coordination is therefore improved. The children have the ability at this age to maintain focus with a significant level of self-regulation. There is a bit less muscular elasticity compared to the previous stage, although elasticity still remains at a high level. Near the end of this stage, which is considered pre-puberty, some of the physical measurements, such as speed, will not be all that far away from where they will be during adulthood.

Boca Juniors wall art - Buenos Aires, Argentina.[10]

---

[10] Photograph: Elemaki – Wikimedia Commons 2006.

12 to 14 years old

PSYCHO-PEDAGOGICAL CHARACTERISTICS:

During the 12-14 stage, puberty begins and is a major factor for the children of this age group. Hormonal changes occur that can bring about changes in character: internal conflicts, questioning of authority etc… The child at this age level demonstrates the ability to assimilate abstract concepts and to objectively evaluate results and performance obtained via concrete evidence. Reasoning overtakes emotions and the child at this age looks for logical justifications.

PSYCHOMOTOR CHARACTERISTICS:

During this stage there are great changes to the child's coordination which can adversely affect his ability to run, jump, maintain balance, control the ball etc… There are also notable differences between the maturation and corporal development between individual players. Some are more physically developed while others have not yet hit puberty. During this period there are rapid morphological changes and maturation of biological structures: systems of control, locomotive apparatus and energetic systems.

14 to 16 years old

PSYCHO-PEDAGOGICAL CHARACTERISTICS:

There are continued hormonal changes that began in the prior stage that can lead to variations in character. The adolescents of this age group have the ability to assimilate and reason abstract concepts of a certain complexity. They have the tendency to question morals and values while seeking common principles and interests when choosing their friends. This group of friends plays an important social role that at times may displace the importance of the family. Attention is given to the future as an important reality and specifically the adolescent's own reality.

PSYCHOMOTOR CHARACTERISTICS:

During this stage there are huge changes in coordination along with noticeable differences in the level of maturation and corporal development between team members. This is mainly due to the variations in the timeline of the growth spurt that occurs during this stage. Some experience the growth spurt earlier while some experience it later. *It is important to take this into account when making player selections. The larger more physical players will tend to dominate physically. The danger exists to leave smaller more intelligent players aside. There is a maturation of biological structures: control systems, locomotive apparatus and energy systems. At the end of this stage, the adolescent's development with regards to height, weight, sexual maturation, will be almost complete.

⚽ A rythmic warm-up at the Tahuichi Academy in Santa Cruz, Bolivia.

PEAK HEIGHT VELOCITY – GROWTH SPURTS

Children develop physically at different times and at different rates, and this means that we will have a mix of early, average and late developing athletes on our teams. It is essential that a coach understand when these growth patterns occur. In order to better understand the growth patterns of our players, a coach must be aware of Peak Height Velocity (PHV). This is especially true since the patterns for males and females occur at different times and rates. Normal growth stops when the growing ends of the bone fuse. This usually occurs between the ages of 13 to 15 years for girls and 14 to 17 for boys. See the following chart.[11]

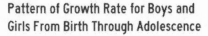

Pattern of Growth Rate for Boys and Girls From Birth Through Adolescence

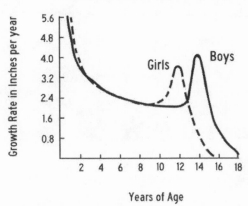

Years of Age

---

[11] Article: Long Term Athlete Development – Published by the Canadian Sport Centres.

According to the article <u>Long Term Athlete Development</u>, published by the Canadian Sport Centres, PHV occurs in females at around twelve years of age while boys hit their PHV on average around 14 years of age. During PHV, the boys grow an average of 3 ¾ and 4 inches per year. In around four years the average boy grows approximately eleven inches. On average the girls grow around 2.5 inches the first year of accelerated growth, followed by 3 inches the second year, and around 2.5 inches the third year for an average of around 8 inches. Once the PHV is achieved, a period of deceleration occurs. Normal pubertal growth is characterized by three stages: acceleration, deceleration and cessation.

Due to such extremely accelerated growth rates, some players end up with a painful condition called Osgood-Schlatter disease. Although more common among boys than girls in the past, the data shows that girls are now afflicted at nearly the same rate. The disease refers to the inflammation of the bone and surrounding soft tissue just below the knee. It generally occurs at the same time as a player's Peak Height Velocity, but can happen anywhere between the ages of 9-16. Coaches for this age level need to be aware of the symptoms of Osgood-Schlatter, and if necessary, adjust training sessions to avoid heavy amounts of running on cement or very hard ground. This may mean bypassing the road run up hills in order to do more technical training where there is not so much pounding on the knees. Sometimes a player will be affected by the pain so much that he will need to stop soccer altogether and do alternate training such as biking or swimming. Extreme growth spurts can also cause a player to lose coordination, balance and speed. If unresolved it can be painful, of considerable duration, and have a permanent negative effect on the bone. This can jeopardize a young athlete's potential.

Finally, coaches must be aware of mental burnout. Overtraining is the root cause of players burning out, with some of the symptoms including chronic pain, fatigue and decreased performance. In its most extreme form, it can lead to a child quitting sports altogether. This type of burnout at a young age can turn children off to sports and can lead to difficulties with self-esteem, disappointment and a complete rejection of sports for life. For this reason it is critical that coaches understand their players psyche as well as their growth patterns. They must be observant, good listeners and have the ability to differentiate the experience for each player whenever possible. Coaches must also strive to make training enjoyable, reduce the number of excess tournaments, and focus mostly on the positive rather than on mistakes in order to avoid having more children drop out of youth sports.

CHAPTER 6

Helping Maximize Potential

"A good coach is one who helps his players maximize or discover their potential. That is his principle function." – <u>Marcelo Bielsa</u> (Coach of Athletic Bilbao and former Coach of Argentina and Chile)

Inspiring the players and bringing out their passion for the game and for life is one of the most important jobs that a coach may have. In order for a coach to inspire his players to go above and beyond where even they believe they can go, it is important to understand the way each of them approaches the process of learning. There is no doubt that children are complex and unique, having lived lives of varying experiences and backgrounds. Despite this fact, when it comes to approaching learning, Stanford professor Carol S. Dweck PH.D., in her book, <u>Mindset</u>, writes that human beings tend to fall into one of two categories, a fixed mindset or a growth mindset. Dweck explains that those who fall into the fixed mindset category, tend to believe that the amount of talent they have is predetermined. They are convinced that no matter how hard they work, they will never make considerable improvement. Soccer players with this type of mindset are constantly trying to prove themselves and have real difficulty dealing with making mistakes. According to Dweck's book <u>Mindset,</u> these type of people avoid taking risks so they can minimize the number of mistakes they make. Dweck writes that the major reason behind this fear of taking risks is how fixed mindset people equate making mistakes with failure. She goes on to explain how children who view the world this way, no matter how talented, tend to end up seeing themselves as failures and in many cases never reach their true potential.

"Fear defeats more people than any other one thing in the world." – <u>Ralph Waldo Emerson</u> (American Author)

Players with a growth mindset, on the other hand, believe that with hard work and effort, anything is possible. They understand that making mistakes is just part of the process of learning and improving. These players tend to take more risks and allow themselves the chance to develop their creative side. They understand that effort is the key to improvement. The good news, according to Carol Dweck, is that mindsets are not set in stone and can be changed with encouragement, teaching and guidance.

It is fascinating to know that this difference in mindset only begins around ten years of age. According to Darren Treasure P.H.D., Assistant Professor of Sport and Exercise Psychology at Arizona State University, research shows that children under the age of 10 equate ability with effort. He states, "Because young children cannot differentiate effort from ability, they do not have the cognitive ability to understand winning and losing." This is the reason why the youngest players do not come off the field worrying about the score or who won or lost the game. They are more interested in finding out what kind of snack they will get, or if they will be going to the playground next to the field. From ten years of age and onward, children begin to define success in two different ways. Some continue to see the path to success through improvement and effort (growth mindset), while others begin to approach life in a more adult oriented way in which they are constantly comparing themselves with others. This leads players to an unbalanced focus on outperforming others where winning becomes the major focus (fixed mindset).

"Failure happens all the time. It happens every day in practice. What makes you better is how you react to it." – Mia Hamm (Two-time World Champion for the United States women's team)

So how do some children end up with a fixed mindset where they avoid making mistakes at all cost, and they fear failure? According to Dweck, many children grow up receiving constant praise from their parents and coaches. Comments such as "This is so easy for you.", or "You are the most talented player out there." should be replaced by "You must have worked hard to master this skill.", and "Your work ethic has helped you to improve as a player." Children who are reminded daily that they are "extremely talented" begin to believe that everything should come so easy for them. The majority of this praise is directed towards the youngster's talent rather than on the effort that led to others to see him as talented. This type of praise that focuses on talent and not on effort often leads the child to believe that talent is something that is predetermined and that hard work is not linked to improvement. This of course is the farthest thing from the truth. The great Pelé stated, "Success is no accident. It is hard work. Perseverance, learning, studying, sacrifice and most of all love of what you are doing or learning to do."

When players come to us, we must be conscious of the fact that some will not believe that they can get better through effort, and they will fear making mistakes. This holds true for all skill levels from recreational level all the way up to Development Academy youth teams. It is part of our job then as coaches to encourage, teach and construct an environment conducive to developing a growth mindset. When it comes to creating a training environment in soccer, it is important to allow players to take risks and try out new ideas. This is extremely important with regards to player development since we have yet to develop large numbers of highly creative players in this country. It is a must that coaches talk to players about how making mistakes is ok and, that it is just part of the process of becoming a better player. The legendary John Wooden wrote in his book, They Call Me Coach ,"The team that makes the most mistakes will probably win." "The doer makes mistakes, and I wanted doers on my team—players who made things happen. Players who are afraid to make mistakes generally do not take risks and do not make things happen."

So how can a coach begin to nurture the growth mindset in training sessions? Firstly, a coach should have ongoing discussions with the entire team as well as individual players about the differences in mindset. One may also have the team participate in activities that encourage players to play as aggressively as possible with no fear of failure. This will require players to put out maximum effort and then be rewarded them with praise for their all-out attempt, even if they fail.

Another way to encourage such creativity is by holding practice sessions where there is no coaching and only free play. In this situation, those players who are normally fearful of making mistakes, when the coach is running the practice session, will have the chance to play in a worry free environment. In this environment players will be less preoccupied with making mistakes and will take more risks. While running the training session a coach should also be aware of the type of comments he makes to the players. Comments should praise effort and hard work a high percentage of the time. This will encourage the players to focus on the importance of these aspects of their lives.

"If you always put limits on everything you do, physical or anything else. It will spread into your work and into your life. There are no limits. There are only plateaus, and you must not stay there, you must go beyond them." – _Bruce Lee_ (Legendary Martial Arts Expert)

A program such as I-Soccer, that measures specific technical ability, is a concrete way to help players see that their efforts are linked to improvement. For this reason, technical ability should be measured periodically throughout the year. This will help improve motivation and will lead to more practice time and, in turn, an improvement in technical ability.

One example of an activity that I have used frequently for measuring technical skill in a concrete manner is having the players walk with the ball while juggling from the end line to the edge of the 18 yard box and back over a period of 5 minutes. Each length achieved is equal to 1 point. If this activity is done throughout the season, a coach can make an informal assessment about the improvement of each of his players in one area of controlling the ball. The message regarding different mindsets and the importance of praising effort must also be communicated to parents, so that there is a clear message coming from home that success in any aspect of life has a direct link to effort and hard work.

To me it is clear that if we do not make an effort to better understand the way our players think, and begin to encourage a growth mindset, then we will continue to see players drop out of the game or never reach their true potential.

☆ Captain of World Cup Champion Japan and Female 2012 World Player of the Year – Homare Sawa.[12]

---

[12] Photograph: GNU Free Documentation License - Wikimedia Commons 2011.

CHAPTER 7

Developing Talent

"If you distill all the new science about talent development into two words of advice, they would be practice better." – Daniel Coyle (Author of – The Talent Code)

So what does it take for soccer players to acquire talent? Although some believe that it is innate and that great players are born talented, other top youth coaches such as Laureano Ruiz in Spain, assert that soccer players are made, not born. He believes that players do not just become talented overnight without putting in thousands of hours of practice time. Let's take a look at the definition of skill and how players go about developing it. The term "skill", when referring to a soccer player, refers to the ability to decipher when, where and how to realize a specific technique within the game for the benefit of one's team. It is important to keep in mind that having great technique (dribbling, juggling, ball control) does not necessarily make a great soccer player. In order to develop such skill, a soccer player must be placed in an environment where he repeatedly reaches beyond his comfort zone and is challenged, makes mistakes, adjusts and corrects the mistakes. This ultimately leads to the player's improvement. In the eyes of knowledgeable coaches, the best teacher in the sport of soccer is the game itself. For this reason, the soccer coach as a general rule should stimulate the players by creating the correct environment and by guiding the training. He should do what he can; however, to avoid continually interrupting the overall flow of the session. When one states that the game is the best teacher, the reference is not directed solely to the 11v11 game. In fact the ideal environment for developing great soccer players must come in a progressive form of small-sided games that <u>maximize,</u> through repetition, situations in the game where the player uses perception, decision making and technique to solve problems. (*see chapters on small-sided/global games and futsal.) The environment must be one that matches the tactical sophistication level of the players in order to challenge them without being either too overwhelming or overly simple.

Daniel Coyle, author of <u>The Talent Code</u>, spent time investigating why Brazil is a so called "hotbed" for soccer talent. What he discovered is that the game of futsal, along with the Brazilian's passion for the sport, (which leads Brazilian children to play for hours at a time every day) create the perfect combination for talent growth. (*see chapter on creativity.) Without ignition, something that ignites the player's inner drive and passion, there is no direct path that will lead to mastery of a skill. The two must be present in order for talent to be developed.

🜨 A futsal court in Petrópolis, Rio de Janeiro – Brazil.[13]
Another arena for developing talent.

---

13 Photograph: Eduardo Pazos - Wikimedia Commons 2012.

Coaches who seek to guide the development of talent in youth soccer players first must understand <u>what</u> a quality practice environment looks like (*see the chapter on training sessions.) while also being aware of what is actually happening in the athlete's body when this type of practice is taking place. Daniel Coyle refers to this type of quality practice as "deep practice." In order to truly understand how talent is nurtured and developed, coaches should also focus on the <u>how</u> and <u>why</u> of talent development.

According to researchers in neuroscience such as Dr. George Bartzokis, professor of neurology at UCLA, the insulation that wraps around and insulates nerve fibers called "myelin" is the basis for learning new skills. For example, each time a soccer player perceives what is happening in a game, makes a decision and executes a movement in soccer, he builds more myelin insulation which in turn helps the efficiency of the transmission of information through the neurocircuits of the brain. The more myelin that is built up, the stronger, faster and more fluid our movements and thoughts become. *(see diagram on page 82) When youngsters are exposed to futsal or small-sided/global games where there are many decisions to be made and much more contact with the ball, they are building much more myelin insulation than in the 11v11 game. As a result, they are building a deeper skill base. In Coyle's book <u>The Talent Code</u>, Dr. George

Fields of the Laboratory of Developmental Neurobiology at the

National Institutes of Health at Bethesda, Maryland explains this

process a bit further. He states "All actions are really the result of

electrical impulses sent along chains of nerve fibers. Basically our

brains are bundles of wires called neurons connected to each other by

synapses. Whenever you do something, your brain sends a signal

through those chains of nerve fibers to your muscles."

The process of sending signals to the muscles has two parts. The

first part is the input, or all that happens before one performs an action.

(Perceiving what is around us and the actual decision) The second part

is the output path which refers to the execution of the decision.

(Running, passing, shooting on goal etc...) See graphic below:

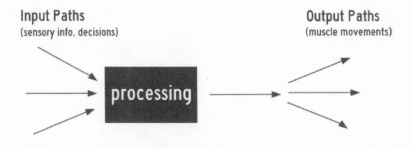

In the diagram below, one can see where the myelin insulation is built up in the myelin sheath of a neuron.

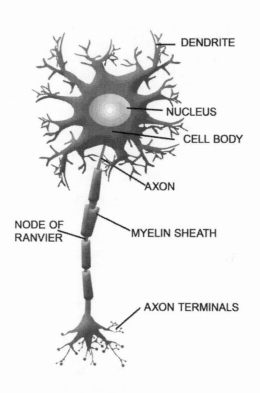

"It doesn't matter where one is born. What is important is what and where one learns... and with whom."

– _Ramon Maddoni_ (Youth Coordinator at Boca Juniors)

Coyle, in his conversations with Dr. Fields came to realize that there are two essential ingredients to building myelin and in turn creating talent. These ingredients are the following:

✪ TWO MAIN INGREDIENTS FOR DEVELOPING MYELIN AND SKILL.

1. The best way to build a good circuit, and in turn build myelin, or skill, is to <u>fire it over and over again</u>, <u>correct mistakes</u> and <u>fire it again</u>. Some ways to create this situation include: futsal and small-sided/global games. Wise soccer coaches understand that they must recreate street soccer as much as possible at their training sessions and allow their players to learn from the game.

2. Since building up a huge circuit with myelin insulation takes so much time and energy output - 10,000 hours for mastery of a skill, in order to do what it takes to become great, one must have a <u>deep love or passion</u> for the sport or activity. What can light this fire? It is obviously different for each child. Some possibilities include: culture, a soccer first family, a parent's passion, a friend's passion, an inspiring coach, positive soccer experiences, soccer on television, competition etc…

The steps of the learning process.

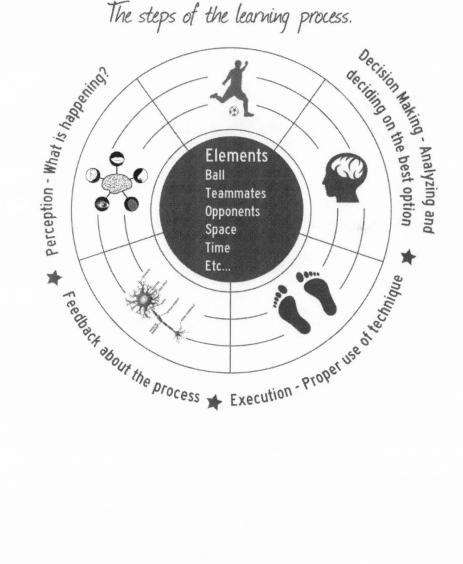

Perception - What is happening?

Decision Making - Analyzing and deciding on the best option

Execution - Proper use of technique

Feedback about the process

Elements
Ball
Teammates
Opponents
Space
Time
Etc...

CHAPTER 8

Player Selection

"Players are chosen to enter La Masia at Barcelona based upon three criteria: technique, the ability to understand the game, and mental speed. Physical strength and height are given no importance whatsoever." – Marti Perarnau (Author of <u>Sendas de Campeones</u>)

The way the player selection process is viewed in many places in the United States, with emphasis on big, tall, physical players, together with the emphasis on winning, we are no doubt losing a lot of late bloomers before they even have a chance to develop. Players who are smaller and not as strong have difficulty competing against those who are more physically developed; therefore, they stay on the bench and do not end up playing very much. This leads many of them to become discouraged, to stop enjoying themselves, and to leave the sport altogether. The importance that has been placed on winning only fans the flames and encourages coaches to seek out players who are physically dominant who can help them win games, rather than on players who may be of a smaller, slighter stature but who are highly skilled. Anyone who disputes the fact that people of any size or stature can play the game of soccer at the highest level need look no farther than Barcelona in Spain where Leonel Messi, Xavi Hernandez, and Andrés Iniesta, are all 5'7" tall. In fact, many other great players of all time are at or under this height. They include: Maradona, Roberto Carlos, Andrea Pirlo, Romario, Edgar Davids, Zico, Ferenc Puskas, Garrincha, Abedi Pelé, Omar Sívori, Pablo Aimar, Gheorge Hagi among others.

So what are the main criteria for selecting players to enter Barcelona's youth training center La Masia? Former Olympic Athlete, and author of the book, <u>Senda de Campeones</u> (Path of Champions), Marti Perernau, has spent considerable time living in Barcelona and studying how player development works at the player development center known around the world as La Masia. According to his findings, the three traits most sought after by scouts looking for players to bring to train at La Masia include 1. technique, 2. tactical intelligence, and 3. mental speed. When asked how much emphasis Barcelona puts on physical size and strength when it comes to player selection, he answers "none".

We must pause for a moment and ask an important question. Would it even have been possible for players such as Messi, Xavi, and Iniesta, to have developed in the kind of system found in many places in the United States? At this point it is clear that the answer is "no".

Vicente Corral – Scout

On the following pages, the Spanish scout Vicente Corral, details what he looks for when searching for a future professional soccer player. In Spain Vicente Corral is considered an expert analyst in the recruitment of talented soccer players. He has worked as a soccer analyst and scout, discovering new footballing talents while collaborating with various well known digital newspapers such as Marca.com and Goal.com. Vicente also collaborates with most of La

Liga teams including Real Madrid, Barcelona, Sevilla, and Villareal among others - compiling and sending reports on talented players.

INFORMATION PROVIDED BY VICENTE CORRAL:

Technical Skills:

For me these are the most important skills for becoming a professional soccer player. I look closely at the area around the ball and the skills related to it. If a player does not stand out in this area, it can be difficult for him to excel in soccer. We all know specific cases in which a player reaches the professional ranks based on strength and desire to become a professional, but to reach the elite level one must have some outstanding technical skills, including among the individual or collective technical skills the striking of the ball with the foot, head, dribbling, shooting on goal, ball control, passing, combinative actions, feints, etc. ...

Mental and Physical Speed

Speed is another one of the most important skills a player can have, and it can be defined as the ability to move as quickly as possible.

When I say speed I'm thinking about all kinds of speed that are important to a soccer player, the reaction time, sprinting speed, and especially the <u>mental</u> speed that influences, decision making and execution. Also worth special mention is acceleration which directly measures the rate of change of speed. Acceleration capacity is another important skill that a soccer player must have. It has less to do with speed over long distances, in soccer it is important to be very fast over short distances of 5-10-15-20 meters, where a split second can decide whether or not a goal will be scored. Virtually all elite players have this ability to accelerate. Other skills needed are physical strength, coordination, jumping power, endurance, flexibility, agility, etc ....

Tactical Skills

From age 13 onward is the right time to start intensely working the tactical aspects of the game. After this age the player is better able to understand complex tactical situations and has the cognitive ability to make the proper decisions on the field. A player's perception and peripheral vision is also important to read the game as it unfolds. The offensive skills that can be named include: support, change of speed, creating spaces, playing rhythm, timing, etc ... The defensive skills include: pressing, marking, cover, tackling, anticipation, etc ...

Behavior

The way a player comports himself can give many clues to the scout regarding the possible future of a player. I look at how the player behaves among his peers, with his coach, and even the opponents. Does he have a positive attitude? Is he brave, is he disciplined, does he have self-confidence and trust other's actions? Is he a leader in team? Does he maintain concentration, and does he have the ability to overcome adversity? Does he communicate well with peers? Does he have organizational skills? Well, there are many hints that the players provide on the field that can help in the final decision about the future of a player.

Once I am clear about the player's abilities, I will be in a position to analyze his shortcomings and possible solutions, and more importantly, mentally visualize the evolution that the player may have over time. It seems to me essential to become informed regarding a wide variety of areas that may affect the player and not only areas based on sport. I also look at the extracurricular activities he is involved in, the sports background of parents, injuries, family illnesses, family environment, school environment, hobbies, etc .... all information which can give you the key to knowing how that player will develop in the future and assess whether he will have a real chance of one day becoming a professional soccer player.

CHAPTER 9

Creativity

Young players need freedom of expression to develop as creative players... they should be encouraged to try skills without fear of failure.
— Arsene Wenger (Manager of Arsenal)

In a lecture on creativity given for Media Arts in 1991, John Cleese[14] talks about the research on human personality done by the scientist Donald W. MacKinnon at U.C. Berkeley during the 1970's. The research showed that a person's level of creativity has no direct relation to IQ. And while society tends to see creativity as a talent, McKinnon points out that this assumption is simply not the case. Cleese asks the question "what then exactly is creativity"? In answering this question he credits McKinnon's research for defining creativity not as an ability that one has or does not have, but instead as a way of operating. Cleese explains that people who are most creative are the

---

[14] John Cleese - English comedian, author, and lecturer.

ones who have the ability to tap into their natural ability to be childlike and to play. Mackinnon's research, according to Cleese, showed that the most creative people had the ability to delve into play by exploring ideas that had no immediate practical purpose or meaning, and were done just for enjoyment. He also states in his lecture that the biggest adversary of creativity is the fear of making a mistake. When relating this to soccer, it is clear that the street, backyard, or free play soccer environment is where creative players are born. These are the places free of stress, where players feel a certain freedom to play and try out new things without worrying about making mistakes and being criticized. These games are not timed, and the players are able to immerse their entire state of being in "the game".

Both John Cleese and psychiatrist Dr. Robin Skynner, agree that there are two modes in which people tend to operate in life. These can be broken down into the "open" mode and the "closed" mode. According to Cleese and Skynner, creativity is simply not possible in the "closed" mode. On the following pages I have listed the characteristics of the two modes. The first list contains characteristics of the "closed" mode where creativity tends to be stifled, and the second has characteristics of the "open" mode where creativity is allowed to flourish.

CHARACTERISTICS OF THE "CLOSED" MODE

1. Structured, there is work that we must get done

2. Anxiety, tension and stress are present

3. More fear of failure

4. We are impatient

5. Not much humor

6. Everything is done for a purpose

"Our goal is to create a stress-free, comfortable soccer environment.
It's all about playing, not about results or suffocating them with tactics
and systems. It's just one step away from the playground."
- Manny Schellscheidt (Former Youth United States National Team Coach)

CHARACTERISTICS OF THE "OPEN" CREATIVE MODE

1. Relaxed and less structured

2. Less purposeful

3. More playful

4. Less fear of failure

5. A place to try out new things

6. No pressure to get something done

When contemplating the development of creative players in the United States, the question that must be asked is the following: How often do our youth soccer players find themselves in an environment that allows for creativity, as opposed to an environment where creativity is stifled? If creativity is so vital to player development, than we must do what it takes to find ways for our players to be in an environment where creativity can flourish.

REQUIREMENTS FOR GETTING INTO THE "OPEN" MODE ACCORDING TO <u>JOHN CLEESE</u>.

1. Space (one must separate from routine daily life)

2. Time (one must not be rushed and paying attention to time)

3. Confidence (one must not fear making mistakes)

4. Humor/Joy (one must be in a playful mood where things are not too serious)

Even though children are born with the disposition to be creative, they tend to lose this openness to creativity as they move into adolescence and then into adulthood. The main reason for this shutting down of creativity may be in large part due to the lack of opportunities where they have space, time, no worries about making mistakes, and the joy to play. The great Spanish artist Pablo Picasso was quoted saying "All children are born artists." The challenge as soccer coaches, is to find ways to allow players to tap into what is already a natural desire to be creative. Helping the creativity in our children to surface is not an easy proposition; however, since our schools, and every other part of our structured society, allow so little time for play and creativity.

There is no doubt that in places where unorganized free play still exists, creative players are still being developed. Generally when one thinks of creative soccer players, one thinks of players from Africa, South America as well as the countries in southern Europe. Of course free play exists in most parts of the world including the United States on varying scales largely depending on the neighborhood. It is not something that is being nurtured; however, by our structured "club" environment. I would venture to say that this statement would hold true for our Academy System. We must begin to address this situation in the United States even if it means thinking and doing things completely differently than we have in the past.

🌐 One of the most creative teams of all-time - "La Maquina" (The Machine) of River Plate of the 1940's in Argentina. (Carlos Muñoz, José Manuel Moreno, Adolfo Pedernera, Ángel Labruna, and Felix Loustau)[15]

---

[15] Photograph: Wikimedia Commons 1941 – Argentina copyright expired.

CHAPTER 10

Player Development Recommendations: An Appropriate Progression

"Children will only learn quickly, effectively and thoroughly when the demands of the training sessions or competitions they participate in match their intellectual, psychological, and motor skills." – Horst Wein (Author and internationally renowned coaching mentor)

It has not been until fairly recently that youth soccer development has become a focus around the world. For many years even in the world's top soccer countries, there was no time or financial support given to youth soccer development. Of course in the United States, these Academies have only recently been established or are still in the process of being formed. It had long been thought that soccer training should be approached the same for both the adults and the children. This premise has since been proven to be incorrect. Despite the formation of professional youth academies, our present model continues to fail our young soccer players. If we continue on the same path as we always have, the results will be more players dropping out of youth sports due to frustration and a lack of enjoyment along with the poor preparation of our athletes to compete at the highest levels.

With regards to appropriate complexity and progression, I believe it is worth looking at what has been proposed by the United States Soccer curriculum, compared to the recommendations of other authorities of youth soccer development around the world. On the following pages I have provided information regarding player development and appropriate complexity from some experts around the globe. The information comes from author and internationally renowned coaching consultant Horst Wein of Germany, former Barcelona Youth Academy Director Laureano Ruiz of Spain, Enrique Borrelli of (ATFA) the Argentine Football Coaches Association, and the English F.A.

✪ United States Soccer curriculum: stages of development and recommendations for age level complexity in games.

Stages of development: Initial stage, basic stage, intermediate stage, advanced stage, specific stage, and senior stage.

Initial Stage: 5-8 years olds Number of Players: 5-6 years old, (3v3), 7 years old (4v4), 8 years old (7v7) Formation: none recommended	Advanced Stage: 15-18 years old Number of Players: 11v11 Formation: 4-3-3 and 4-4-2
Basic Stage: 9-12 year olds Number of Players: 9v9 Formation: 3-2-3	Specific Stage: 19-20 Number of Players: 11v11 Formation: 4-3-3 and 4-4-2
Intermediate Stage: 13-14 year olds Number of Players: 11v11 Formation: 4-3-3	Senior Stage: 21 and above Number of Players: 11v11 Formation: 4-3-3 and 4-4-2

🌐 Information provided by United States Soccer Curriculum.

Opinion: According to Horst Wein (see following pages), the progressions recommended by the United States Soccer Curriculum are still too difficult and complex for the assigned age groups.

🌎 United States Soccer Federation Headquarters – Chicago, Illinois.[16]

[16] Photograph: Permission Wikimedia Commons 2007.

Perhaps the leading authority in the world regarding player development in soccer is the German Horst Wein. He has written numerous books on the subject, and his methods have been advocated by top international managers such as Arsene Wenger at Arsenal. In 1986, after observing him coaching field hockey, the legendary Spanish winger Carles Rexach brought Wein to Barcelona to put on coaching clinics for the 29 members of the Barcelona coaching staff. Since then he has gone on to mentor coaches at many top clubs around the world such as Inter Milan, Nacional, Peñarol, Athletic Bilbao among others. It is his belief that player development must be done in a progressive manner that fits the appropriate level of the child's development. He points out that we wouldn't think of teaching our children advanced mathematics such as Calculus at 6 years old; accordingly, he believes that we should not put our youngest players in situations such as the 11v11 game that are far too complex for them to handle. His opinion is that players (ages 4- 6) should begin by playing soccer at home where there is absolutely no pressure, and where they can have fun and experiment with the ball. He also recommends that formal competitions begin after age 9. According to Wein, training sessions should be player centered with open ended questions being asked of the players rather than the coach providing all the answers. His four goal game with scoring zones recreates the street soccer environment and allows for the simultaneous development of perception, decision making and technique.

Horst Wein's stages of his Soccer Development Model and recommendations for age level complexity in games.

Age group: 6 years old and under No formal competition Play at home with a ball.	Age group: 11-12 years old Number of Players: 7v7 Ball Size: 4
Age group: 7-9 years old Number of Players: 3v3 Ball Size: 3	Age group: 13 years old Number of Players: 8v8 Ball Size: 4
Age group: 10 years old Number of Players: 5v5 Ball Size: 4	Age group: 14 and up Number of Players 11v11 Ball Size: 5

🌐 Information provided by Horst Wein.

Horst Wein's book <u>Fútbol a La Medida del Niño</u>, (Developing Youth Soccer Players) has been the official textbook on youth development for the Royal Spanish Football Federation (RFEF) since 1993. Horst has also spent considerable amount of time with various professional clubs in Mexico such as Pachuca, Monterrey, Pumas, America and others. A number of Mexican players who recently won the U17 World Cup were introduced to Mini-soccer/Fuñino at an early age. Many of the top clubs throughout Mexico use the textbook mentioned above with their (fuerzas básicas) youth academies.

Laureano Ruiz, from Spain, is a former Racing Santander player who is considered by many to be one of the most knowledgeable coaches in Spain regarding all aspects of youth soccer development. He had an enormous influence on the youth program at Fútbol Club Barcelona where he helped develop the style of play that exists today at the club. He was the first to introduce the rondo exercises at training sessions at Barcelona, and he changed the player selection focus from physical attributes such as height and strength to game intelligence and technique. Some of the players he helped to find and develop include "Lobo" Carrasco, Rojo, Moratalla, Calderé, Munitis, Ivan Helguera and Ivan de la Peña. He is held in high regard by the Dutch and Barcelona icon Johan Cruijff who in the 2009 Spanish documentary, "el Fútbol Fútbol" stated "Laureano is someone who doesn't overly focus on winning matches at the youth level. He instead focuses on the long term development of his players." Cruijff goes on to mention how Laureano's teams have won various championships, but they did so while playing "real" soccer. In Laureano's development model, there are four basic stages. In the first stage the players learn to play with the ball. In the next stage they learn to play with teammates. In the third stage they learn to play against opponents, and in the fourth and final stage they learn to improve speed of thought and decision making.

Laureano Ruiz's stages of development and recommendations for age level complexity in games. (Former head coach and youth program coordinator at F.C Barcelona.)

Stages of Development: 1. Learn to play with the ball, 2. learn to play with teammates, 3. learn to play against opponents, and 4. learn to improve speed of play.

<u>Learn to play with the ball</u> Age group: 8-10 years old Formation: 1-2-1 Number of Players: 5V5 Pitch: 40 x 28 yards Ball Size: size 3 ball	<u>Learn to play against opponents</u> Age group: 13-14 Formation: 3-2-1-2 Number of Players: 9 v 9 Pitch: Regulation Size Ball Size: Size 4
<u>Learn to play with teammates</u> Age group: 11-12 years old Formation: 3-2-1 Number of Players: 7v7 Pitch: 68 x 50 yards Ball Size: Size 4	<u>Learn to improve speed of play</u> Age group: 15 and up Formation: 4-3-3 Number of Players: 11 v 11 Pitch: Regulation Size Ball Size: Size 5

☆ Information provided by Laureano Ruiz.

Argentine Football Association

Over the last few years Argentina has surpassed Brazil as the largest exporter of soccer talent in the world. Some of the world's most talented players such as Maradona, Leonel Messi, Sergio "Kun" Aguero, Hernan Crespo, Gabriel Batistuta, Javier Pupi Zanetti, Omar Sívori, Jorge Valdano, Angel Di Maria, Juan Román Riquelme, Daniel Passarella, Carlos Tevez and many others have developed their game in Argentina. According to Boca Juniors Youth coordinator Ramón Maddoni, players are scouted for Boca Juniors at Club Parque in Buenos Aires very early on and brought into the club as young as 6 years old. On the following page is information on the stages of development and recommended age level complexity for games. It is interesting to see that in structured environments in Argentina the game is played with larger numbers. On the weekends ten year olds are playing 11v11 soccer. The influence of futsal and street soccer is still there. According to Enrique Borrelli of Club Atlético Independiente, futsal is even more popular in the interior regions than it is in Buenos Aires.

---

* Although Argentina continues to develop world class players, the progression used in competitions is still too complex for each age group. Enrique Borrelli at Club Atlético Independiente admits that the numbers for weekend games is too large, and Horst Wein is of the same opinion regarding AFA's recommended age level of complexity in games. What seems to make the difference is that the average Argentine Youth player still spends a tremendous amount of time in pick-up games, and practicing with a ball outside of the structured training sessions.

Argentine Football Association - AFA stages of development and recommendations for age level complexity in games.

Age group: 7/8 years old Number of Players: 8 and a keeper Field Size: 70 x 45 yards wide Ball Size: 4 Duration: Two 20 min periods Goal: 5 x 2 yards	Age group: 11-13 years old Number of Players: 11v11 Field Size: Regulation Ball Size: 5 Duration: 2 periods of 30 minutes Goal: Regulation
Age group: 9 years old Number of Players: 8 and a keeper Field Size: 80 x 50 yards wide Ball Size: 4 Duration: Two 20 minute periods Goal: 5 x 2 yards	Age group: 14 years old Number of Players: 11v11 Field Size: Regulation Ball Size: 5 Duration: Two 35 minute periods Goal: Regulation
Age group: 10 years old Number of Players: 11v11 Field Size: Regulation Duration: Two 25 minute periods Ball Size: 5 Goal: Regulation	Age group: 15 years old Number of Players: 11v11 Field Size: Regulation Ball Size: 5 Duration: Two 40 minute periods Goal: Regulation

Information provided by Enrique Borrelli – ATFA Instructor and Youth Coordinator at Club Atlético Independiente Buenos Aires, Argentina.

F.A. Adopts New Development Proposals

On Monday 28th May 2012, F.A. Shareholders voted in new Youth Development proposals by an overwhelming 87 per cent majority. The Shareholders, present at the AGM at Wembley, voted to bring in a new player pathway for football to include a mandatory 5v5 format of football for U7s and U8s and a 9v9 format for U11 and U12s to be phased in by season 2014-15.

The changes passed have been developed over a number of years, with research and over two years of consultation across the game. Nick Levett, National Development Manager, said: "After 138 roadshows nationwide it was fantastic to get the endorsement of the majority of the grassroots football community. "These changes are a massive step forward for the future of children's football in this country."

Introducing 5v5 for U7s and U8s, with progression to 7v7 and then 9v9, allows the children to play on appropriate size pitches and with appropriate size goals. The smaller pitch and number of players allows greater number of touches of the ball and involvement in the game, helping develop greater technical skills at a lower age. The move will also bring a more child friendly approach to competition, breaking up the eight-month long adult based season into smaller periods of competition which encourage increased learning.

<u>Dermot Dalton</u> – General Manager "The Beautiful Game." 6/03/ 2012

F.A. Football Association of England.

Age group: 7/8 years old Number of Players: 5v5 Field Size: 30x20m and 40x30m Ball Size: 3 Goal: 12'x6'	Age group: 11-12 years old Number of Players: 9v9 Field Size: 70x40m and 80x50m Ball Size: 4 Goal: 16'x7'
Age group: 9-10 years old Number of Players: 7v7 Field Size: 50x30m and 60x40m Ball Size: 4 Goal: 12'x6'	Age group: 13+ years old Number of Players: 11v11 Field Size: Regulation Ball Size: 5 Goal: Regulation

Information provided by Dermot Dalton, General Manager of "The Beautiful Game" www.thebeautifulgame.com

* According to Horst Wein, the new progression of competitions for youth football in England is better than it was, but not yet correct and still too difficult and complex for the assigned age groups.

Soccer -7 (7v7)
(one reason for Spain's success)

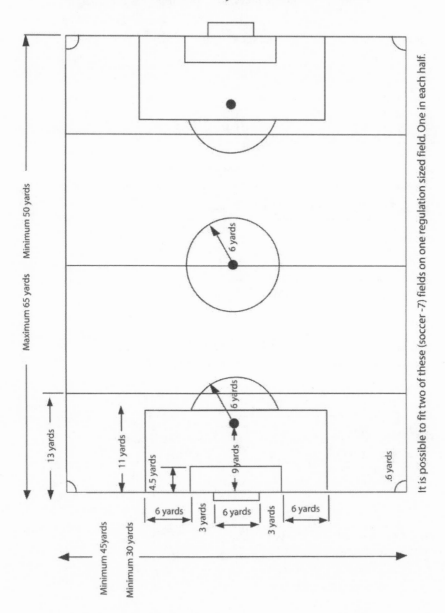

Minimum 50 yards

Maximum 65 yards

6 yards

6 yards

13 yards

11 yards

4.5 yards

9 yards

6 yards

6 yards

6 yards

3 yards

3 yards

.6 yards

Minimum 45yards

Minimum 30 yards

It is possible to fit two of these (soccer -7) fields on one regulation sized field. One in each half.

In Spain, youth players are placed in a progressively complex game format with youngsters playing in the (Soccer - 7/Fútbol - 7) or 7v7 format until age 12. According to Cristian Catena, a youth coach at the Benjamin (U-10) level at F.C. Barcelona, one of the major reasons for the success at Barcelona and with the Spanish National Team is the fact that they have incorporated the 7v7 game into their curriculum. When asked about the benefits, he pointed directly to the fact that the players have increased involvement in the game with both technical and cognitive benefits. In fact, there is such an importance placed on the (Soccer-7/Fútbol -7) format at Barcelona that they even have a coordinator dedicated entirely to the 7v7 game. The next time you have your manager schedule a friendly with a local team, you may want to have your team play in the 7v7 format. More players are on the field at one time. Here is a list of some of the benefits:

1. Smaller goals 6x2 yards benefit goalkeepers who now can have many more successful actions instead of playing with a goal size meant for an adult.
2. Quicker thinking in smaller spaces. More one touch passing.
3. More emphasis on the technical over the physical.
4. More cognitive decisions in 2v1 situations. (the atom of the game)
5. More transitions in the game (from attacking to winning the ball back and vice-versa)
6. More contact with the ball, more shots on net, more goals scored and more fun!

CHAPTER 11

The Coach

"The coach is first of all a teacher." – John Wooden

COMMONALITIES AMONG TOP YOUTH SOCCER COACHES

While recently observing some of the most successful youth programs around the world, United States Youth Technical Director Claudio Reyna noticed some commonalities between the coaches working at these clubs. When referring to the style that these coaches employed during training sessions, he is quoted saying "The coaches were guiding the training and not stopping play for every mistake." The importance of allowing the play to flow without focusing on every mistake helps player development in a variety of ways. First it lowers the anxiety levels in order to allow for better focus and more learning, and second it allows the player to adapt and solve problems on their own within the constantly changing environment. It is clear that for better soccer development, coaches should focus on stimulating more and coaching less. The key, according to author Daniel Coyle is that the type of skill circuitry that a soccer player is trying to build needs a certain adaptability to the changing environment with perception, decision making, technique and improvisation all playing a part.

According to Daniel Coyle, author of the Talent Code, (*see chapter on developing talent) when observing "master coaches" of various sports in different parts of the world, he also noticed some consistent traits.

1. Vast and deep knowledge
2. Perceptiveness and the ability to listen
3. Short bits of important information (No speeches)
4. High moral standards – especially empathy

The first commonality he noticed was, despite the importance of being prepared and always having a plan, was the ability of the coach to spot teachable moments and to do effective spontaneous coaching that made the difference. The coach with a vast and deep knowledge is generally able to see more. This allows for more in depth coaching points.

The second characteristic of a "master coach" is the ability to be perceptive and to listen more than talk. The ability to learn things about a player's state of mind, comprehension, motivation, and dedication is a vital skill for a coach to manage. Those coaches who listen to others are much more likely to gain their pupil's respect, and in turn are more likely to guide their student towards maximizing their potential. Perceptive coaches are able to notice differences in each of the players which allows them to approach each individual a bit differently. For example, some players need a bit more of a push, while others need a pat on the back. This perceptiveness also relates to how much a coach is able to see when observing his pupil perform. It is not always an easy skill to develop and takes many years of practice to do it well.

The following are some things that make a good listener. Firstly, a good listener uses eye contact appropriately, is attentive and alert to a speaker's verbal and nonverbal behavior, is patient and doesn't interrupt (waits for the speaker to finish). is responsive, using verbal and nonverbal expressions, asks questions in a non-threatening tone, paraphrases, restates or summarizes what the speaker says, provides constructive (verbal or nonverbal) feedback, is empathic (works to understand the speaker), shows interest in the speaker as a person, demonstrates a caring attitude and is willing to listen, doesn't criticize, and is nonjudgmental and open-minded.

The third trait that Coyle observed in master coaches was their ability to not overwhelm the student with long lectures. They interceded only when necessary and they imparted specific corrective feedback. The play was allowed to flow with few stoppages. Most of the coaching points made by the observed futsal "master coaches" were done within the flow of the practice by asking questions of individual players who had recently made a mistake. There was no excessive focus on mistakes, and points were made only when deemed important enough to do so. In fact, most of the time, the futsal coach relied on the game to provide the coaching points. A good soccer coach recognizes that players learn from the game and from each other more than from the coach.

The final trait that these "master" coaches had in common was that they all had a quiet and reserved personality. They didn't run around crazily shouting instructions and telling their pupils what to do. Since soccer is an "open" sport, with an infinite number of changing situations and problems to solve, the best coaches, when interacting with players, try to allow them to think for themselves without handing out all the answers. The personality of these coaches is also characterized by empathy and selflessness with the focus on making a connection with each and every one of their pupils.

🌐 A Club Atlético Independiente training session with Américo Gallego.

CHAPTER 12

The Training Session

"The ideal training session is that which reproduces the intensity and the emotions of competition." – Telê Santana

TRAINING METHODS

In the pursuit of developing a possession oriented attacking style of play, it makes sense to focus in on the world's top proven training methods such as those used at F.C. Barcelona. It can easily be said that no one else in the world at this moment has had as much success in producing such a style of play as has F.C. Barcelona and the Spanish National Team. In fact, it could be said that these teams have changed the way that we look at soccer around the world. According to youth coaching coordinator at F.C. Barcelona – Sergio Vallecillos Sánchez, the training methods employed at Barcelona's Youth Academy – La Masia include a variety of rondos, possession games, positional games, other small sided games, mixed with some analytical practice. (*see chapters on rondos/positional games, small-sided/global games, perception etc… for training ideas) The topics employed at training sessions at Barcelona are part of a long term development curriculum that is not derived from the previous weekend's game. There is always a plan in place that serves the long term development of the players and the coaches teach the predesigned curriculum. *Players are encouraged to play the ball on the ground and are not allowed to just kick the ball out of play or to mindlessly send the ball long up field with no purpose.

PERIODIZATION AND ANNUAL EDUCATION PLANS

In top training sessions around the world, the top clubs and coaches optimize learning by being extremely well planned. This helps maximize training time while also teaching the concepts that have previously been decided upon as being the most important for player development at each age group. The curriculum is laid out by experts at the club and is followed by the coaching staff. The term "periodization" is applied to the planning of training sessions and the arrangement of those sessions in an orderly manner. Each training program is generally broken down into two periods, the preparation period and the competitive period. The training program is further broken down into microcycles = weekly plans, mesocycles = monthly plans, and a macrocycle: yearly plan.

The following are brief descriptions of each from ATFA:

- A <u>microcycle</u> is by definition the shortest training cycle, typically consisting of one or two weeks with the goal of facilitating a focused training block. Two or three microcycles are generally tied together to create a mesocycle.

- The <u>mesocycle</u> represents a specific block of training that is designed to accomplish a particular goal. This mesocycle might consist of 3 weeks of training. Mesocycles are typically 3 to 4 weeks in length but can be a bit longer.

- The <u>macrocycle</u> consists of all 52 weeks of the annual plan. Due to its length, one generally expects to make some changes to it throughout the year. The macrocycle may be thought of as an "overarching" view of the annual training plan.

One of the most important benefits built into a periodization based annual plan is recovery time. It is something that is generally ignored at most youth soccer clubs in the United States as evidenced by the scheduling of excessive tournaments and multiple weekend games. Without a periodization plan we risk putting our players in danger of short and long term injury.

"Dedication in the training sessions along with planning ... decide results." – Ramón Maddoni (Youth coordinator at Boca Juniors)

Intensity, focus, tempo and competition

Along with planning, learning is also optimized by imposing a lively tempo where the training session flows, and there is little transition time from one activity to the next. In top level training sessions each minute of the session is used to engage the players to the point where they must focus on what they are doing. In this way the players will develop the capacity to maintain concentration levels for longer periods of time that will help prepare them to be successful in game situations. Activities making up the main part of the session should be run with high intensity for short periods of time. According to U14 F.C. Barcelona coach Denis Silva Puig, coaches should have high expectations of the players and they should motivate their players vocally if they see the performance level drop off even in the slightest. Vocal motivation should not be confused with giving instructions to the players.

So what do the top coaches do to maintain high tempo training sessions? Firstly, the coaches should always have some balls immediately available in order to continue the flow of the practice session. Whenever possible, multiple exercises should be set up with equipment ready to go in order to limit transition time. Also to speed up transition time and to encourage ownership of the training session, players should be asked to retrieve equipment in between each activity.

In order to increase the motivation and intensity of the practice session while bringing out the emotions of the game, competition should be included in as much of the training environment as possible.

As part of each exercise, the losing team may be assigned a small task, or they may be assigned more of a task that all players are required to do. The task should never be excessive, and it should never be used in order to humiliate. Examples of tasks: bear crawls, burpies, jumping jacks, hops, push-ups, abdominals etc...

"We only train technique and tactics, not fitness, because they can catch up later." – Albert Benaiges (Former Coordinator of the F.C. Barcelona Youth Academy – La Masia)

The Basic Structure of a Barcelona Academy Youth Training Session[17]

Five Phases:

1) Warm up. This is never done without a ball being present.
2) First Part: Specific technical work.
3) Second Part: rondos, positional games, possession games, exercises with defined positions.
4) 7v7 game with and without the use of neutral players, mini game with three teams (rotation), focusing on the theme of the session.
5) Cool Down: used to create good habits in the youth player.

---

[17] Information provided by Albert Capellas – Former Youth Coordinator F.C. Barcelona

THE IMPORTANCE OF TRAINING TO GAME RATIO

In a recent study over a period of two years, the Football Association and the League Manager's Association in England, conducted a number of visits to development academies of top clubs around the world where they learned the following information about game to training ratio: (see the following page) It is understood that to master a game such as soccer, a player must put in approximately 10,000 hours of training time. If done in the proper way, training is so much more valuable to a player's development than an 11v11 game. Why is this so? We need look no farther than the fact that in a game a player averages approximately 90 seconds of contact with the ball.[18] Looking at the chart on the following page that focuses on training to game ratio, it is clear why we are having a difficult time matching up against national teams such as Spain or Brazil who spend much more time in situations of contact with the ball and decision making.

"Everything is practice". - Pelé

---

[18] LA IMPORTANCIA DEL JUEGO EN ESPACIOS REDUCIDOS - Óscar Méndez Albano 2009.

A STUDY OF TRAINING TO GAME RATIO

Time devoted to Training and Coaching -v- Number of Competitive
Games per season:

Club	Age	Training Sessions (hours)	Games
Ajax (Holland)	U9 - U14: 3 sessions (5hrs) per week		22
	U15 -U16: 4 sessions (6.5hrs) per week		22
	U17 - U18: 6 sessions (9hrs. per week		26
Barcelona (Spain)	U10- U14: 3 sessions (4.5hrs) per week		30-36
	U15- U18: 4 sessions (6hrs) per week		30
Parma (Italy)	U10- U14: 3 sessions (4.5hrs) per week		18-22
	U15- U19: 4 sessions (8hrs) per week		30-36
Inter Milan (Italy)	U12- U18: (5-8 hours per week)		26-38
Sao Paolo FC (Brazil)	U12- U14: 5 sessions (15hrs) per week		28
	U15- U18: 5 sessions (20hrs) per week		36-40

★ What catches one's attention is how many more hours there are in training than in games. Now compare this to most clubs in the United States where training is held on average 2 sessions (3-4 hours per week) with sometimes up to five games on the weekend.

CHAPTER 13

Analytical vs Global Training Methods

"Technique is not being able to juggle a ball 1000 times. Anyone can do that by practicing. Then you can work in the circus. Technique is passing the ball with one touch, with the right speed, at the right foot of your teammate." – Johan Cruijff (Legendary player for Barcelona and Holland)

The practice of an isolated technical skill such as dribbling around cones, is an example of an analytical method of training. While it certainly helps develop the execution of the specific skill, it ignores the development of other vital areas of the game such as perception and decision making. In a scenario that is far better for a player's overall development, the same dribbling skill can be developed by putting players in a game situation with teammates and opponents, and then creating parameters that demand the use of dribbling skills. This way the skill of dribbling is being practiced, but so are the skills of perception and decision making. One such example would be playing a simplified game of 3v3 where in order for a team to score, one of its players must dribble over an end line.

The methodology of training that incorporates opponents and competition in more game-like situations is called the global method. It is important to remember that both of these methodologies, global and analytical, should be used during training sessions; however, the vast majority of practice time, around 90% or more, should be dedicated to activities of the global variety. Here is a list of the characteristics of both the analytical and the global training methodologies.

The Analytical Method (repetition of isolated technique)
(*The coach is considered to be using the analytical method if there are no opponents present.)

1. Allows for many repetitions of the technique being practiced.
2. Does not allow for development of perception or decision making.
3. Player motivation is generally lower than when playing in game situations.
4. Does not involve the emotion and intensity of the game.
5. Uses the left hemisphere of the brain. (non-creative)

"A great pianist doesn't run around the piano or do push-ups with the tops of his fingers. To be great, he plays the piano." – Jose Mourinho (Head coach at Real Madrid)

The Global Method – (a ball, teammates, opponents, rules, space)

1. Allows players to experience a more realistic situation to the game with opponents, teammates and the ball.
2. Allows for the development of perception and decision making.
3. Player motivation is generally high during global or game related activities.
4. Involves the intensity and emotions of the game.
   Uses the <u>right hemisphere</u> of the brain. (creativity)

"There is no question that the drills are needed to better technique, but practicing them without referring to the context of the game or competition is of little value. The learner needs a context." – <u>Horst Wein</u>

★ A table soccer game at the (CBF) in Brazil.

Analytical exercise (left) vs global exercise (right)

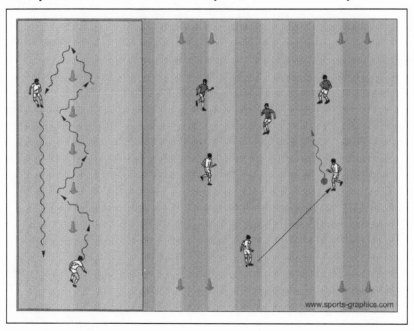

www.sports-graphics.com

☆ On the left (above) is an example of an <u>analytical</u> exercise for dribbling where there are <u>no opponents</u>. The goal is to dribble around the cones and then back to the start. On the right (above) there is an example of a <u>global</u> exercise for dribbling. There is a small-sided 3v3 game to four goals where the focus is on dribbling in a game setting. In order to score a player must dribble through one of two wide goals. In the 3v3 game a <u>ball, teammates, and opponents are all included</u>.

"No two situations are the same in a game of soccer, and this is why players have to develop their technique by actually playing. There is no "ideal" technique; how a player kicks the ball with his instep will always depend on the options available to him, his position on the field, and the positions of his teammates and opponents." – <u>Bert van Lingen</u> (KNVB Coach)

CHAPTER 14

Developing a Possession Oriented Attacking Style of Play

"The intent is not to move the ball, but to move your opponents, that is, I move the ball here (to one area of the field) in order that the opponent is drawn in because at just the right moment when the opponent arrives ... I pass, I pass and I am out of that area. Soccer is that way. Play on the right to end on the left. Play on the left, play backwards, switch the attack, and then end on the right. " – <u>Pep Guardiola</u> (Former head coach at F.C. Barcelona)

As a melting pot of cultures, the United States soccer community is built on influences from all parts of the globe. Some view the game as an art, while others see it as more of a war. These differences in philosophy, the fractured nature of our youth soccer organizations, along with the vast size of our country, have made it more difficult than some smaller countries to come together. Despite these difficulties, as we move forward and seek to improve player development, we should look to develop a common language amongst our players regardless of their age level, background or physical stature that will help them achieve a higher level of play. These areas of common language should include the areas of perception, game intelligence, understanding when and where to execute a movement or technique, mental speed and executing the technique itself. Great soccer players tend to excel in all of these areas.

According to Claudio Reyna in an interview with Mike Woitalla of Soccer America's Youth Soccer Insider Series, everything is tied to style of play. He states that the style of play itself can either help nurture the development of our best players or it can stunt their development. According to Reyna, a player such as Wesley Sneijder of Holland would never have developed into the player he is today if he had been brought up playing an ugly style of play. Reyna states "many potentially great players will be lost in the helter skelter, fast type of (kick and rush) soccer."

A coach must have confidence and conviction in implementing a possession style of play. Many coaches are fearful that they will risk results. Others, through no fault of their own, have not yet learned how to teach the concepts involved. It is essential that coaches put aside any fears and begin the process as soon as possible. For some players it may be too late, but if we ever want to have a chance to develop players who can play at the highest level, we must make the necessary adjustments so that our players have a chance to really take off and fly.

So what is needed to develop an attack oriented, possession style of play? According to the great Argentine coach Jose D'Amico[19], the soccer coach should constantly impress upon his players the importance of possessing the ball along with the following concepts. D'Amico believes that since a team cannot attack without the ball, when possession is lost, it is imperative that everyone help to win the ball back as soon as possible. According to this philosophy, the players should maintain an attack oriented attitude at all times. They should understand that having the ball will give them the initiative to dictate the tempo of play. Keeping the ball also depends on everyone in the team. D'Amico states "When one of our players has the ball, everyone should move to support the player on the ball in order to allow our team to continue the attacking movement." He warns that having possession is not the most important thing, but rather to know what to do with the ball when in possession. Every movement should be for the purpose of helping build the team's attack. He points out that maintaining possession pass after pass does nothing unless there is

[19] Former FIFA Instructor, Argentine National Team Head Coach, Coaching Director ATFA – Argentine Coaches Association, Head Coach at Boca Juniors, River Plate, Vélez Sarsfield, Rácing Club, San Lorenzo, Atlanta, Bánfield and Rosario Central.

ultimately an attempt to penetrate, to open spaces, to move the opponents out of position, to surprise, and to score goals.

A player should always be moving. You can come up with a reason for every player in every position and every circumstance, why he should be moving. In football there is no reason to be immobile." – Marcelo Bielsa (Present coach of Athletic Bilbao in Spain and former coach of the National Teams of Argentina and Chile)

★ Brazilian National Team of 1959 (a year after winning the World Cup in Sweden) with Pelé, Garrincha, Didi, Gilmar, Djalma Santos etc...[20]

---

[20] Photograph: Tito Martens – Wikimedia Commons 2007.

Below is a list of general principles that are in line with the style of play outlined in the United States Soccer Curriculum:

☑ keep the ball, don't lose it

☑ play mostly on the ground

☑ constant support is given to the player in possession of the ball

☑ when in possession move to support the player on the ball.

☑ play from the right in order to attack from the left (disguise intent)

☑ play from wings in order to attack from the middle (disguise intent)

☑ play out of the back

☑ goal kicks are frequently taken on the ground to feet

☑ the goalkeeper frequently throws or rolls the ball instead of punting long

☑ play through the lines

☑ high percentage of throw-ins to feet and back to thrower (use throw ins to maintain possession and to switch the point of attack)

☑ switch the point of attack with speed and precision

☑ team maturity can be measured by the appropriate ratio of back passes.

☑ wingers keep the game wide and deep. "Foot on the line/pisa la linea."

☑ seek numerical superiority in attack. (create 2v1's through overlapping)

☑ if penetration is optimal it should be made.

TELE SANTANA

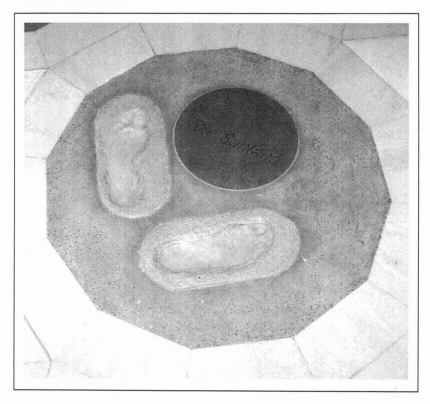

⊕ Tele Santana's footprint inside Maracanã Stadium in Rio de Janeiro. The coach of some of Brazil's most memorable teams at the 1982 and 1986 World Cups. A lifelong advocate for the beautiful game.

CHAPTER 15

Playing Out of the Back

"My only way to interpret the game is that the ball is played on the ground." – Marcelo Bielsa (also see quote – page 129)

One of the measurements of a team that is dedicated to long term development over a win-now approach, is how well they can play out from the back. The term "playing out from the back" according to the U.S. Soccer Curriculum, refers to "The collective action of transferring the ball from the defensive third to advanced attacking areas." Frequently this is action is started through the distribution of the goalkeeper. Teams that rarely play out from the back do not train this during practice sessions and therefore do not risk this type of play in games. Playing in fear of giving the ball away in a dangerous area, these team's goalkeepers are instructed to play the ball long and in the air through goal kicks and punts. Their field players are told to play the ball long up the field or to kick the ball out of play if in danger. Those youngsters who are not exposed to the type of training required to play out from the back, lose out on developing important skills such as passing, control, providing the correct angle of support, composure, perception, and decision making.

Teams that are seeking to develop players over the long term tend to play a possession style of soccer where there is more emphasis on passing and maintaining control of the ball. The training progression, should allow the players to learn the game over time in progressively more complex situations (5v5, 7v7, 9v9, 11v11) and to eventually gain the ability to possess the ball in tighter spaces and under extreme pressure in the 11v11 game.

Leading up to the 11v11 game at U14, players should have been exposed to many hours of rondos (possession games), and progressively complex small-sided games, where they are able to learn perception and correct decision making as well as technique. Once at the U14 age level, despite the addition of 11v11 tactics and functional training, it is important that possession games and small-sided games still be incorporated frequently at training sessions, and that those players weak in passing accuracy or reception, or who have a liability with a "weaker foot", be encouraged to do extra practice playing against a wall. It only takes one weak link to break the whole possession game down. Keeping this in mind when training possession, a coach must recognize the level of his players, and accordingly, adjust the size of the field to create an environment where players are challenged to their maximum, make errors and in doing so improve their game. When a team is training to play out of the back the coach should make it clear that it is unrealistic to play out of the back every time, since there will be occasions when it is simply not the best option. The coach should emphasize that what is more realistic is to have the team play out of the back whenever possible.

So what should it look like when playing out from the back? First, there must be a rational occupation of the space with many passing lines all over the field. In this way there will be constant support for the player on the ball. Circulation of the ball should be done quickly, moving it with speed through many shorter passes that will allow the team to advance as a unit. Next, players need to correctly position their bodies. For example, the players on the outside need to have their backs to the touchline in order to receive the ball while still being able to have a good perspective of the field. Players receiving in the middle must open their bodies and be positioned sideways on to better see the field and to receive facing forward. There must be constant movement of the players in advanced positions searching for spaces in between the opponent's lines. The progression of the team must always be made in a collective manner, with no players making

isolated penetrating runs into space.

In conclusion, the ability to pass the ball out from the back with

success is a product of the proper development training and does not

just happen overnight. On the following pages I have included a

progression of activities with graphics that present ideas on how to train

playing out from the back beginning with 5v5 all the way through the

11v11 game. I have also provided information on the goalkeeper's role.

5v5 Game (2-1-1)

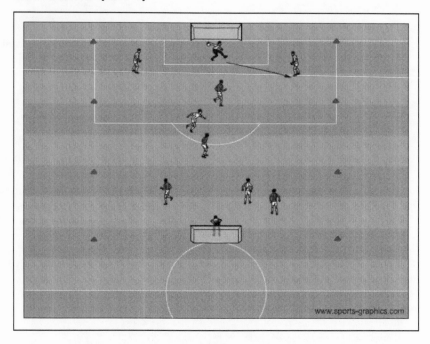

★ In this small-sided game to big goals with goalkeepers, the backs should be encouraged to open wide and deep when the goalkeeper is in possession of the ball. Here the recommended formation is 2-1-1.

7v7 Game (3-2-1)

★ As the game progresses to 7v7 the goalkeeper still has the option of playing out to either of the outside backs, but will also have the option of playing through the center back. Here the recommended formation is 3-2-1.

9v9 (3-2-1-2)

☆ As the game progresses to 9v9 the goalkeeper still has the option of playing out to either of the three backs, but will also have the option of playing out through a center midfield player. Here the recommended formation is 3-2-1-2.

Training - playing out from the back (4-3-3)

1. The coach should first walk the players through the various options for playing out from the back with the team in an 11v0 situation. This must be repeated over various practice sessions (see graphics on the following pages.) The coach should address the role of each player.

Outside the training grounds of Club Atlético Independiente – Buenos Aires, Argentina.

11v11 - Playing out through a center back

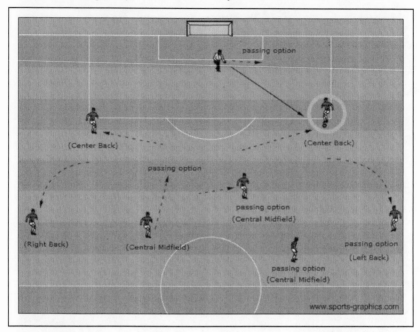

✯ In this situation the ball is played on the ground from the goalkeeper to one of the two center backs. The center back's positioning must be at the corner of the 18 yard box and sideways on to receive a pass cleanly. Possible passing options now include: The goalkeeper, the left back, a withdrawn central midfielder and an attacking center midfielder. In this situation with space in front of him, the center back should, optimally, dribble forward with speed in order to set up a pass.

11v11 - Playing out through a center back (deeper drop)

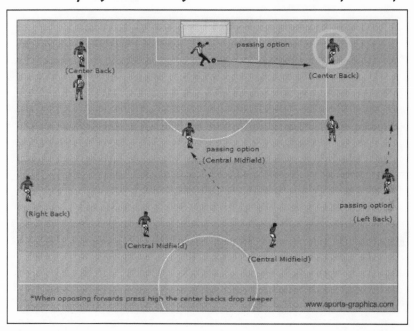

★ If a center back is put under pressure by an opposing forward, then he may drop even deeper to receive a pass. In this situation the ball is passed on the ground from the goalkeeper to one of the two center backs who have taken up an even deeper position due to pressure from an opponent. Possible passing options now include: The goalkeeper, the left back, and a withdrawn central midfielder.

11v11 - Playing out through an outside back (deep)

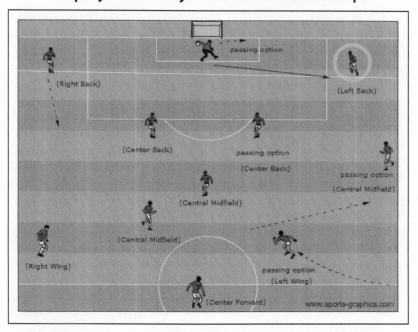

⭐ In this scenario the outside backs have opened wide and deep. (*Notice the position of the center backs is pinched in.) The goalkeeper passes the ball on the ground to the left back. The attacking central midfielder on the side of the ball needs to immediately move out wide to offer a passing option to the left back. Possible passing options now include: The goalkeeper, the attacking center midfielder (out wide), a center back and a left wing who has moved inside to allow a better angle of support to the outside midfielder.

Playing out through an outside back (wide position − midfield line) with center backs dropping deeper.

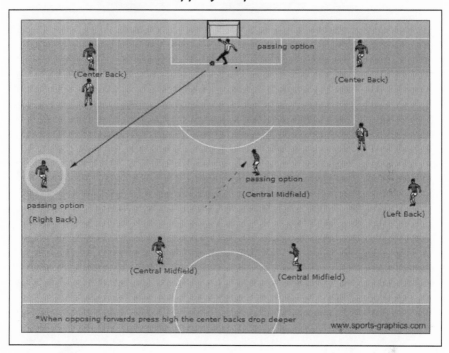

★ In this case, one of the center backs has been put under pressure by an opposing forward. The forward follows the center back into a deep position. This opens up a lane to pass the ball out wide to the right back who is unmarked. Possible passing options now include: A withdrawn central midfielder, an attacking midfielder, and a winger.

Playing out through the center midfielder

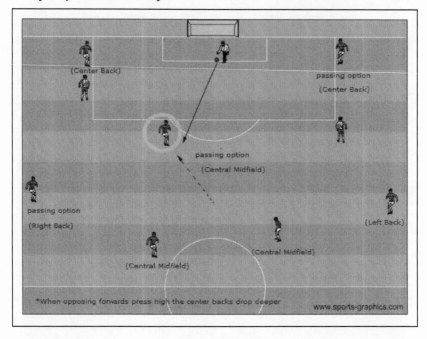

★ In the next scenario, passing options to the center backs are taken away by the opponents. This leaves an option to play out through the withdrawn midfielder. In this situation the ball is passed on the ground from the goalkeeper to the withdrawn midfielder. Possible passing options now include: Both attacking central midfielders, the right back and the left back.

8v3 game

★ After players have seen the various options of playing out from the back, they progress to an 8v3. The team with eight players has a goalkeeper, a back four, and three central midfield players. The team with three has one forward and two deeper lying midfield players. Play begins with a service from the coach (a shot on goal) to the keeper's hands or directly from a goal kick. The objective is to try to build an attack that ends up crossing the half line between either of two gates placed in wide areas. Encourage the players to start on one side and switch the point of attack to the opposite side. Progression: <u>Build up to an 8v4, an 8v5 and then an 8v6 game</u>. (Two forwards and four midfield opponents.)

THE ROLE OF THE GOALKEEPER

When a team plays out of the back, the role of the goalkeeper is critical. According to Horst Wein, 68% of all actions that the modern goalkeeper is involved in, are in building the attack. The goalkeeper is the one who decides when and to whom the ball is played. He is not only responsible for deciding where the ball goes, but he must also provide support once the ball is in play. The goalkeeper's technique in distribution must be accurate and with the appropriate speed in order to maintain possession and to inspire confidence in his teammates. The goalkeeper's perception must also be of high quality as it is directly related to the decision of when and where to play the ball. He must be able to gauge distances of opponents and positioning of teammates before passing the ball. On the next page are important concepts for the goalkeeper when playing for a team that plays out of the back. I have also included some graphics related to training the back pass and distribution on the following pages. These are analytical exercises with no opponents. For more game realistic exercises with opponents involved see beginning of the chapter.

IMPORTANT CONCEPTS FOR GOALKEEPERS WHEN PLAYING OUT OF THE BACK[21]

1. Almost all passes should be made with the inside of the foot.

2. The majority (approximately 85%) of first touches should be made with the inside of the foot and the other 15% with the outside of the foot.

3. When catching in a crowd, the goalkeeper after securing the ball, should run forwards 5 yards while scanning the field in order to see where to distribute the ball.

4. The goalkeeper's priority is to make sure the ball is under his control before distributing.

5. A good first touch away from pressure is vital, and communication to the outfield players must be early and accurate.

6. The visual cues for making a safe pass are 1. a teammate with time and space and 2. (+2) numerical superiority.

7. The goalkeeper should immediately take up a supporting position after distributing the ball around the 18 yard box.

8. Shorter balls around the 18 yard box should be bowled with the hands or passed on the ground just in front of the receiving teammate. Longer distribution (with the hands) should be thrown overhand.

---

[21] Information provided by professional goalkeeper coach Sorin Popovici.

Specific analytical goalkeeper training to help develop passing out of the back

(*see prior exercises for whole team training)

2 touch passing and support

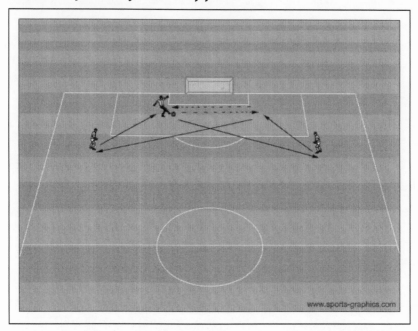

★ In this exercise there is a goalkeeper and two other players. The goalkeeper receives a back pass, makes a good first touch, changes the point of attack with a pass on the ground, and then moves to support the ball. The sequence continues from the other side of the 18 yard box.

4 keepers - one and two touch passing

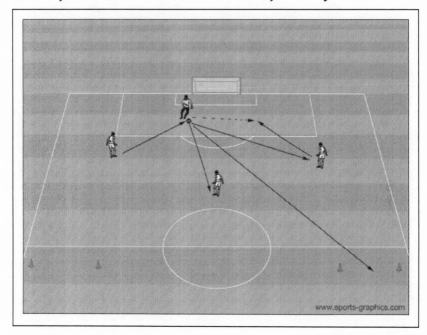

★ In this exercise there is a goalkeeper and three other players. They all pass the ball amongst themselves on the ground - one and two touch. No more than three passes may be made without the ball going to the goalkeeper. After the goalkeeper has made five passes, the next ball must be sent long to a target.

Bowling and throwing practice

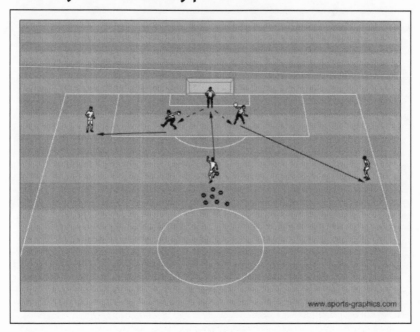

☆ In this exercise the coach has a supply of balls and serves to a
goalkeeper who practices distributing via bowling or throwing to
targets. The targets will move to different places for each sequence.
Keys: Each pass should be made with the proper speed and arrive
accurately and on the ground to the target player.

*Also see chapter on rondos, possession games,
and positional games for even more activities for
developing the goalkeeper's distribution.

🌐 Estadio Monumental – Home of River Plate of Argentina.[22]

---

[22] Photograph: José Porras – Wikimedia Commons 2005.

CHAPTER 16

Playing Through the Lines

"I pass and I move, I help you, I look for you, I stop, I raise my head, I look and, above all, I open up the pitch. The one who has the ball is the master of the game. That's the school of Joan Vila, of Albert Benaiges, of Johan Cruijff, of Pep Guardiola." – <u>Xavi Hernandez</u>

When establishing a style of play based on possession, passing and control of the ball, it is paramount for a team to develop the ability to play through the lines. So what does this entail? When a team plays through the lines it plays from one line to the next (backline to midfield line to forward line) rather than bypassing the midfield. According to studies of the 2006 and 2010 World Cups by Jacob Daniel[23], technical director for the state of Georgia, (using Interplay Sports Software) the top teams in the world such as Spain, Argentina, Brazil, and Germany all play a high percentage of their passes through the lines. To clarify,

---

[23] <u>Playing Through the Lines</u>- Jacob Daniel - United States Youth Soccer National Convention Presentation San Jose, California January 2009.

this means that when the back line of these teams has the ball, they play

over 80% of their passes through the midfield. In the same study,

Daniel found that the United States National Team tends to mostly

bypass the midfield line while playing longer and more direct balls

from the back line to the forward line. He found this to be the case over

80% of the time.

Brazilian U-15 National Team at the (CBF) Training Center.

The Argentinians and other South Americans have a saying in Spanish "pelota dividida" which means a divided or fifty-fifty ball. This type of long forward pass that is less safe, especially if it is lifted in the air, is frowned upon throughout Latin America, and if done excessively, is viewed as anti-soccer. The strategy of winning second balls from longer elevated passes is certainly not one that is conducive to keeping the ball. Since forwards are generally marked closely by the opponent's back line which tends to have numerical superiority, the rate of success in winning second balls tends to be quite low.

Some will argue that the longer lifted balls sent by the United States National Teams in the past were an actual strategy employed by the coaching staff, while others would argue that the root of the problem goes back to how we train and play at the youth level. It is evident that many individual teams and clubs in the United States still employ the win now strategy where longer balls are sent forward to bigger, stronger faster players who can dominate the youth game. When our players are put under pressure at the highest levels and immediately resort to sending long balls, it must be considered that the reason for such action lies in the fact that the players simply resort to what they are comfortable with and have done during their developmental years.

There is no doubt that it is a risky proposition to make a pass from the backline into the midfield that has a chance of being intercepted or stolen. At the youth level a long ball over the top with a run and chase mentality can produce excellent results in terms of winning games. This is where a coach sticking with the long term development model over a win now model is so important. Even if we know that the majority of our players will never see the light of day at the international level, we must teach all our players how to succeed at the highest levels.

A final point to consider when focusing on our team's ability to play through the lines is the ability of our midfield players to frequently receive the ball in positions where they are facing forward. The main advantage of playing through the midfield is obviously that the passing distances are shorter; thus, diminishing the chance for a poor pass or interception. It is important to note; however, that playing from the backline to the midfield line is simply not as effective if the midfield player receiving the ball is unable to get into a forward facing position.

"Short and to feet". – Alfredo Di Stéfano (Former legend of River Plate, Real Madrid, Argentina and Spain)

A player in the midfield line facing forward with the ball is in a position to play a penetrating pass that may develop into a scoring chance. Playing the ball back at times in order to maintain possession is no doubt good soccer, but if it happens too frequently, the opportunities for penetrating passes and the creation of scoring chances will substantially diminish.

On the following pages, I have provided graphics that illustrate various methods of playing from the backline through the midfield line based on the 11v11 game and a 4-3-3 system of play. I have also included graphics of various activities that may be used to teach playing through the lines.

★ U-15 Boys national coaching staff (CBF) Training Center - Brazil.

Centerback runs forward into a midfield position.

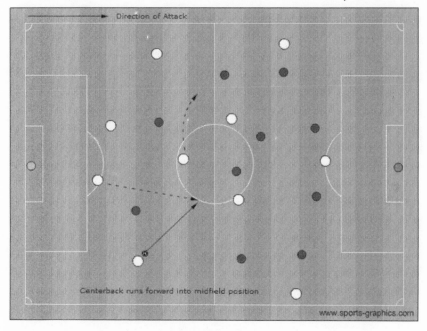

Centerback runs forward into midfield position

www.sports-graphics.com

★ Here one of the two center backs makes a run into the midfield and receives a diagonal pass from the outside back.

Diagonal ball from backline to midfield line.

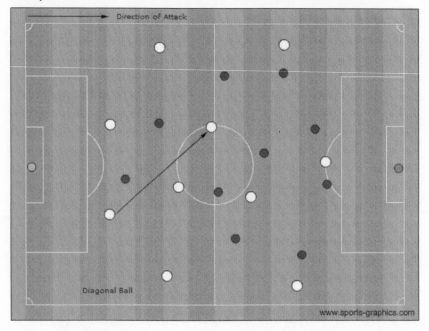

✷ In this situation, one of the center backs makes a diagonal pass to an attacking midfield player.

Dribbling from the backline to set up a pass.

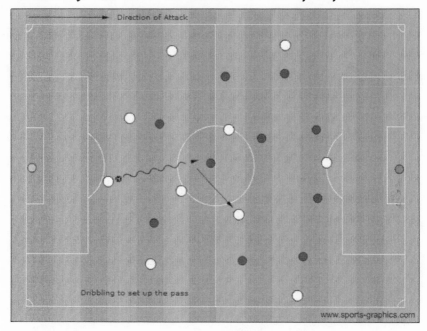

★ As Gerard Piquet often does with Barcelona – one of the center backs dribbles into the midfield to set up a pass to a midfielder.

Forward checks back to midfield to receive a pass.

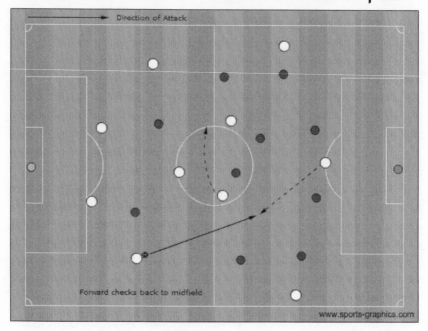

⭐ In this scenario, the center forward checks diagonally back into the midfield to receive a pass from the outside back. The ball is still advancing line by line with a shorter length pass.

Split pass.

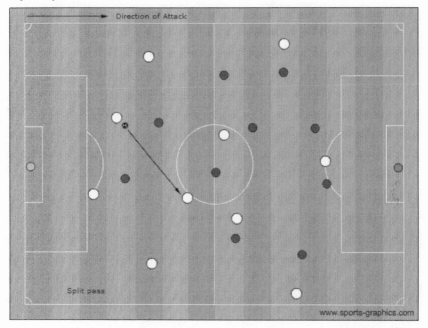

★ On this occasion, one of the center backs makes a diagonal pass to the withdrawn midfielder splitting two opponents.

Switching the point of attack.

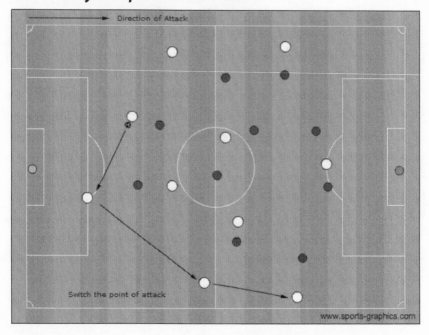

★ Here the ball is switched from one side of the field to the other. As the ball is switched across the backline, it goes to the right back who has taken up a position in line with the midfield.

TRAINING TO PLAY THROUGH THE LINES (4-3-3)

(6v6+Neutrals Possession Game)

★ In this game, played on <u>one half of a field,</u> there are two teams consisting of three midfield players in the central zone and one forward in each of the end zones. There is a 7 yard buffer zone between the central zone and each end zone. There are also 6 neutral players (2 sets of two outside backs plus 2 goalkeepers) who help the team in possession. The objective is to play from one side to the other from the back line to the midfield line and then to the forward line. Once this is achieved the attack goes back the other way. When the outside backs receive the ball they are encouraged to dribble into the central zone (creating 4v3 situation) to set up a pass to a midfield player. The back then immediately takes up his original position.

<u>Coaching points:</u> Always try to penetrate when optimal. Draw the opponents in and switch the point of attack.

(8v8 + 1 Neutral Midfielder)

★ In this game, played on <u>one half of a field</u> to regulation size goals, there are two wide zones for four wing backs. (2 from each team) The wing backs may only attack and cannot defend. Each team consists of a goalkeeper, two center backs, two central midfield players (plus a neutral midfielder) a forward and two wing backs. There are three zones, a defensive zone, midfield zone and attacking zone. Players must stay in their assigned zones until the ball is played to one of the wing backs. When the wing back receives the ball he may dribble into the attacking zone. One attacking midfield player may also go into the attacking zone. This creates a 3v2 situation.

<u>Coaching Points:</u> Backs should open wide immediately when keeper is in possession. Don't hesitate to use the goalkeeper when needed. Always seek penetration when optimal. Draw the opponent in before passing.

<u>Progressions:</u> 1. Wide players may defend in the midfield zone. 2. Wide players may defend in any zone. 3. All players may move anywhere.

164

(9v9 Three Zone Game)

★ This game is played by 18 players (including goalkeepers) in a <u>70x40 yard field</u> split the length split into three zones of 25, 20, and 25 yards. The goalkeeper starts the play by playing to a back. The back in less than three touches must try to connect a pass with a midfielder. If successful, the back may join the midfield to create a 4v3 situation. When a midfielder receives a pass from a back, he has three touches to play to a forward. Again if successful he may join the forwards in the final third. The forwards have unlimited touches before shooting at goal. No player may dribble the ball into a new zone. When a movement is ended, the players reset to their original positions.

<u>Coaching Points:</u> The focus is on making supporting runs into space. Chances should be created both in central and wide areas.

<u>Progressions:</u> 1. Any player may run forward into a new zone once the ball has been played in. 2. Play 11v11 on a full field still divided by three zones.

ANALYTICAL PASSING EXERCISES FOR BUILDING THE ABILITY TO PLAY WITH ONE TOUCH

(*Analytical exercises should only be done for short periods of time with the majority of practice time dedicated to global or game-like situations.)

Diagonal/layoff

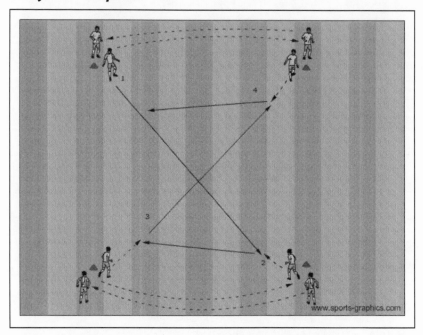

☆ In this exercise there are four cones stationed in a 20x15 area. Two players are on each cone. The ball starts with a diagonal pass and then a one touch layoff. All touches throughout the exercise are <u>one touch</u>. The players do not go across but rather change sides so as to allow them to practice using both feet. Start with one ball and then increase the challenge by progressing to two and then three balls. (7 minutes.) *This exercise is for players who are ready for one touch passing.

166

4 boxes passing

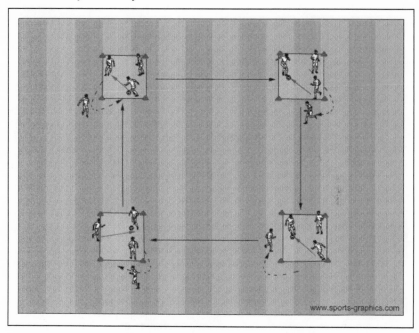

★ In this exercise there are four 10x10 yard boxes placed 20 yards apart. Four players in each box pass one touch and move around a cone. The ball should not stop. The exercise is good for <u>one touch passing,</u> <u>proper body angle for supporting the ball</u>, and <u>moving after the pass</u>. (7 minutes - longer with progressions)

<u>Progressions</u>: 1. Pass the ball clockwise from one grid to the next. 2. Pass the ball clockwise and then follow the pass. 3. Dribble out of the box (clockwise) and play a wall pass with someone from the box that is receiving the ball. 4. Dribble out of the box and play an overlap with a player from the box that is receiving the ball. *This exercise is for players who are ready for one touch passing.

Dutch box passing

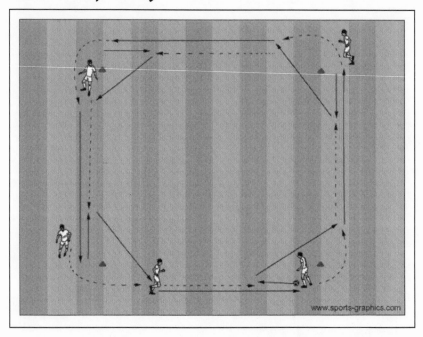

★ In this exercise there is a 15x15 square. (5 players total per square) Two players on the starting cone and one on each of the other three cones. The sequence is the following: (longer pass/layoff/spin around cone/short diagonal pass/spin around cone – then the sequence continues around the box) This should be built up to where it is done with considerable speed and accuracy. *This exercise is for players who are ready for one touch passing.

Circle Perception Passing (multiple balls)

www.sports-graphics.com

★ In this activity the players spread out around the center circle. Three players (center midfield players) are in the center. Players on the outside have one touch and players in the middle have two touches. Encourage players to fill open spaces and to move elsewhere after the pass. Start with two balls and then add a third. Place extra balls close by to maintain the flow. <u>Coaching points</u>: look early, constantly scan the area, if you are in the middle - look over your shoulder, show at a diagonal and receive sideways on in order to facilitate turning, keep the ball on the ground, communicate, move to the ball, move after the pass.

Trenzas (The weave)

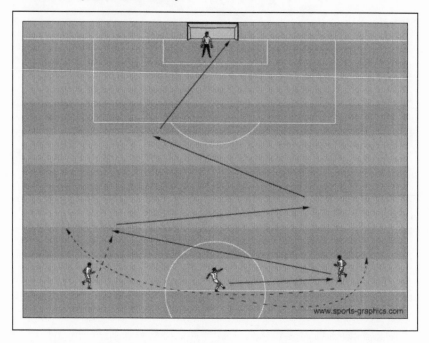

★ In this exercise there are three lines of players stationed at the half line. The middle player begins by passing to either the right or left and then overlapping with a change of speed. The receiving player plays one touch and then continues the overlapping sequence. The player receiving just outside the 18 yard box shoots at goal. All passes are one touch and should be timed to arrive just ahead of the receiving player running into space. All overlaps should be done at speed being careful not to run ahead of the pass before it is played. Each run must come from behind the ball. This exercise is good for one touch passing, passing and moving, timing and accuracy of the pass into space, and finishing. After the third pass the next group goes. (7 minutes) *This exercise is for players who are ready for one touch passing.

CHAPTER 17

Developing Independent Thinkers

"If being told how to play enabled children to master soccer we'd have an excess of great players and superb teams." – Mike Woitalla (Soccer America Magazine)

✷ Coach "Kleiton" in a conversation with Cristiane during a training session at Santos Futebol Club, Sao Paolo, Brazil.[24]

---

[24] Photograph: Enrique Arévalo 2011.

The role of the coach has changed over the years, and for the modern youth soccer coach to keep up with the times, there must be a certain adaptation made to these changes. In our society, the traditional coaching role has in the past been mostly coach centered with the source of all information coming from the coach with no input or dialogue from the players. This is now known to be a less effective way of teaching and learning in the game of soccer.

"There is more focus on the content of what we are teaching rather than on how we are transmitting the information." – Antonio Fraile (Doctorate of Education – University of Valladolid, Spain)

According to Horst Wein, instead of the modern coach being a technical-tactical coach who tells his players what to do during all situations in the game, he has become more like a teacher who creates an environment that stimulates the players while guiding them to understand what they are doing and why they are doing it. The modern coach does not concentrate solely on teaching isolated technique, nor does he give all the answers to tactical questions. Since soccer is an "open" (*see chapter on perception for a definition.) and dynamic sport, it is impossible for the coach to control everything during training sessions and games. Instead he creates situations that allow the

173

players to learn from appropriate game-like situations. In this way the player is improving perception, game intelligence and execution of the technique all at one time. The larger goal is to allow the players to be independent of the coach where they don't rely on anyone but themselves to solve the problems presented in the games. According to Horst Wein, statistical analysis shows that after a three month period, players who are instructed, remember about 18% of what is instructed to them, in contrast, players remembered 68% of what they experienced on their own.

"The genuine coach generates ideas and opens the mind of his students. His far-reaching task is to let them think for themselves instead of thinking for them. This means that the coach grants certain freedom to his students, using effective questioning to help them to resolve problems and make decisions." _ Horst Wein (Author and internationally renowned coaching mentor.)

Since the single best teacher is the game itself, it is essential to encourage the players to listen to what the game is telling them. Most of what is learned will come from making decisions, recognizing errors, and correcting errors within the game. When interacting with players; however, coaches should attempt to use open-ended questioning. These types of questions generally begin with words such as "what", "when", "how" and "why".

Examples of open-ended questions

1. <u>What</u> is the advantage of creating a 2v1?
2. <u>When</u> is the best moment for the player in possession to pass the ball to a teammate?
3. <u>What</u> happens when you pass the ball behind a teammate running into space?
4. <u>How</u> can you help your teammate be successful when passing him the ball?
5. <u>How</u> can dribbling at the opponent help in making an overlap successful?

The coach should ask pertinent questions that are related to a recent problem in the game. It is also important to ask single questions and to avoid run-on questions that lead to frustration and confusion. After asking a question, the coach should make sure to allow the player time to think before answering. After listening to the player's answer, the coach may then follow up with another question that helps the player to clarify his answer. Examples: Can you restate that? Could you clarify that further? What are some alternative answers?

Some steps for assisting in the development of independent thinkers

1. Create an environment where the players are playing the game at an appropriate complexity.

2. Allow the play to flow and coach during a break.

3. Encourage players to listen and learn from the game.

4. Encourage players to ask questions.

5. Ask players open-ended questions beginning with what, when, how, why?

6. Allow players time to think after asking them a question.

7. Follow up on a player's response by asking another question leading to a clarification of the answer.

8. During games - refrain from yelling instructions from the touchline.

9. Communicate with parents about the disadvantages of them yelling instructions from the touchline during games.

DIDI

🌐 The great Didi's footprints inside Maracanâ Stadium – Rio de Janeiro, Brazil. He was one of the world's most elegant and creative soccer players who captained Brazil to World Cup titles in 1958 and 1962. (Didi is pronounced gee-gee)

CHAPTER 18

Teaching Important Concepts

Angles of Support

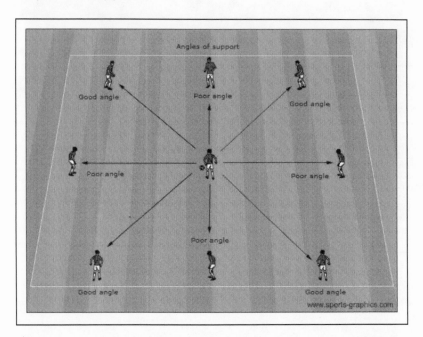

★ One of the most important concepts to teach is proper angles of support. Taking up a position at a 45 degree (diagonal) angle is better than being directly in front or behind or directly next to left or right at straight angles.

Opening "into the light" – Laureano Ruiz

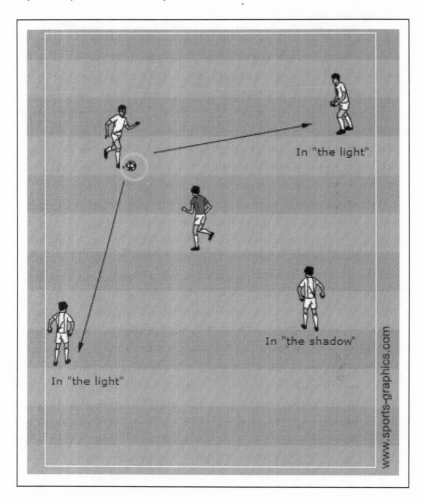

In "the light"

In "the shadow"

In "the light"

www.sports-graphics.com

★ In the above graphic two of the players in possession are correctly supporting the player with the ball. They have taken up a position "in the light." – meaning that they are in a position to receive a pass from the player with the ball. The third player is said to be "in the shadow" as he is not in a position to receive a pass.

Correct body position

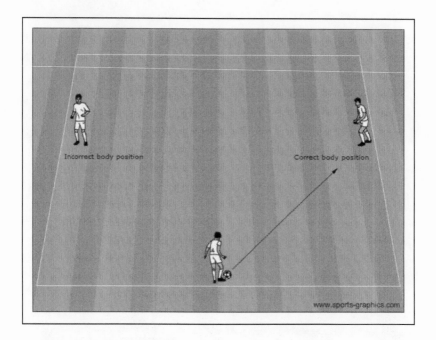

✭ The player on the left has not taken up a good body position to receive a pass. He has limited vision of the field and cannot turn easily when receiving a pass. The player on the right has taken up a better body position. He is open to the field with his back to the touchline and a better view of what is happening around him. He can more easily receive facing forward if the ball is passed to him. It is essential that players be taught how to receive in one motion across the body so they are in position to make the next movement.

Running from behind 2v1 (overlapping) with the player on the ball facing forward.

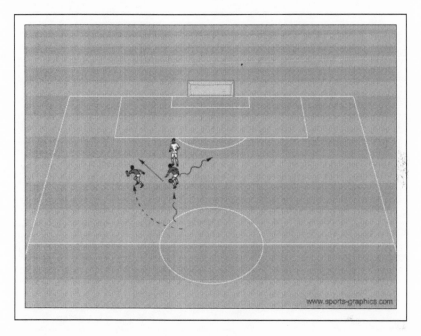

★ When executing an overlap it is important that the player with the ball engage the defender before passing the ball off to the overlapping teammate. This will truly allow for a 2v1 situation where the opponent is in doubt about which way the attacker will go with the ball. According to Horst Wein in his book <u>Funiño</u>, the 2v1 situation is the smallest component of the full game and occurs in soccer approximately 3 times per minute, or almost 300 times in each game. Few players even recognize the 2v1 while playing.

Running from behind 2v1 (overlapping) with the player on the ball back to goal.

www.sports-graphics.com

✯ In this situation the advanced player receives a pass with back to goal. Another player overlaps and creates a 2v1 situation allowing the forward to either lay the ball off with the outside of the foot or turn and dribble in the opposite direction.

After a diagonal a straight – Cesar Luis Menotti

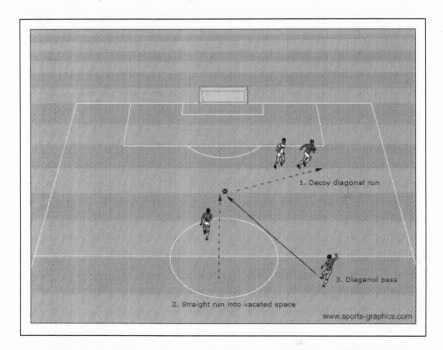

1. Decoy diagonal run

2. Straight run into vacated space

3. Diagonol pass

www.sports-graphics.com

✮ There is a distinction between losing one's mark and making a decoy run. When a forward makes a diagonal run, it is often done as a decoy. If the opposing team's defender continues marking him tightly he will not be in a position to receive the ball facing the goal, and most of the time he will end up playing the ball backwards. After a forward makes a diagonal <u>decoy</u> run in which the central defender is pulled out of position, a midfield player should make a straight run into the space vacated by the forward. If the ball is then given to the midfield player running from behind, this midfield player will be facing forward and in a much more dangerous position.

Disguise intent

✮ There are numerous ways to disguise intent and it is important for coaches to point out how important it is to the players. <u>A few ways to disguise intent include:</u> Looking one way and passing another, lifting the arms to fake a shot or a pass, passing with the outside of the foot, after taking one step toward the ball (pretending to receive it) – letting it run, turning and running on to it, turning the body one way to imply you are going that way and then taking the first touch in a different direction, dribbling fakes such as step over etc…

Opening the field

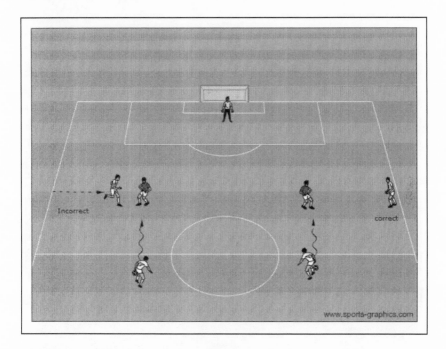

★ On the <u>left</u> side of the graphic above, the wide player has made the decision to run in towards the center of the field. This decision is incorrect as it allows the opponent to neutralize two players. It also takes away the wide option where there is more space. On the <u>right</u> side of the graphic the wide player has made the correct decision not to invade his teammate's space and to open the space by maintaining a wide position.

If I check away I will come to, and if I check to, I will go away ("Si voy es que vengo y si vengo es que voy" - Menotti)

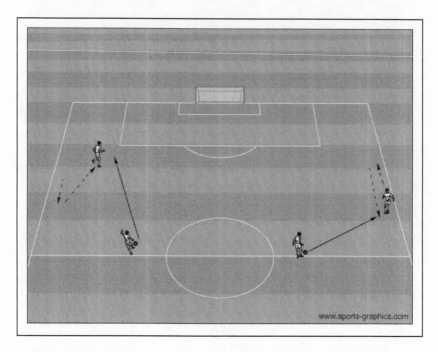

★ On the <u>left</u> side of the graphic above, the wide player has made a short checking run toward the ball to draw the defender closer, and then checks away expecting the ball to be passed into space. On the right side of the graphic above, the wide player has made a short checking run away from the ball and then checks back to the ball. The visual cue of where to pass the ball is given by the player without the ball. Check away first = I want the ball short. Check towards the ball first = I want the ball into space. *The receiving player initiates the pass. The check must be sold properly and done with a change of speed.

Take the first touch toward where you will make the next pass.

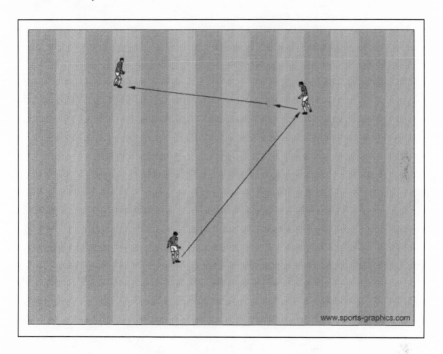

★ In order to improve speed of play and to avoid slowing down the tempo of the ball, it is important to take the first touch in the direction where the player with the ball will make the next pass.

"Doblada" runs – Laureano Ruiz

★ Here are two separate "doblada" runs. On the right the ball is passed to a wide area and then into space for a forward to run on to. On the left, the pass is also made into a wide area and then the passer makes a longer run and gets the ball back behind the defense. These are important ways of gaining penetration in attack.

Wall pass and end-line

★ On the <u>left</u> there is an example of a wall pass. It is important to teach players the proper steps of the wall pass. 1. Engage the defender (dribbling) 2. Pass to a teammate 3. Explode past the opponent 4. Receive the pass into space. On the <u>right</u> is an example of a player facing a 1v1 situation at the edge of the 18 yard box. It is important to encourage our players to not play the ball backwards if they have a 1v1 or 2v1 situation. The players should be encouraged to get to the end-line and seek a cross behind the defense.

CHAPTER 19

Warming Up the Spirit

"The number one reason a child comes to practice is to play."
– Karl Dewazien (Director of Coaching – California North)

Keeping in mind that the primary reason our youth come to practice is to play and enjoy themselves, it is essential to honor this during our sessions. Mixing in a variety of games during the warm up is a fantastic way to get the players moving and warming up while at the same time creating an environment where the players are enjoying themselves. Mauricio Marques, Brazilian Staff Instructor at the EBF

(Escola Brasileira de Futebol) at the CBF Brazilian national training center outside Rio de Janeiro, makes a point of emphasizing the importance of players entering the training session in a "joyful" frame of mind. As part of the level 1 Brazilian Youth License he includes a number of these types of games. Notice that in not one of these games is a player eliminated from the play. Here are a few examples.

BALL TAG

HOW TO PLAY: In this game there are two teams each with a
Brazilian rubber ball. (Rubber playground balls may also be used.) The
two teams pass the ball amongst themselves with the hands and try to
gain points by throwing the ball and hitting an opponent on the back =
3 points or on the shins (below the knees) = 1 pt. Teams keep track of
points and play for rounds of three minutes. The team with the most
points after the two minute round is the winner.

MATERIALS: cones, pinnies, rubber or plastic balls.

AREA: This game may be played in a pre-marked area such as half of
the 18 yard box or cones may be set out in a 25x25 area.

OBJECTIVE: Warm-up and liven the player's spirit, perception,
support of the ball.

CIRCLE TAG

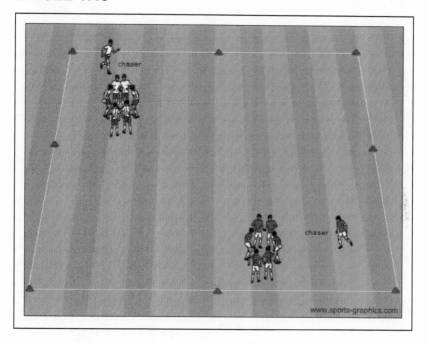

HOW TO PLAY: In this game there are two teams that hold hands and form a circle. One member of each team (in each circle) must tuck a pinnie in his shorts. Each team has a designated "chaser". The chaser's job is to chase down the opponent's circle and grab the pinnie. The circle may run and spin to avoid the capture of their pinnie. The team that first gains possession of the opponent's pinnie wins.

MATERIALS: cones, pinnies.

AREA: This game may be played in a pre-marked area such as half of the 18 yard box or cones may be set out in a 30x30 area.

OBJECTIVE: Warm-up and liven the player's spirit.

HULA HOOP TAG

HOW TO PLAY: In this game there are 2-3 players with a hula hoop. All other players start with a ball on one end of the 18 yard box. On the word "go" the objective is to dribble past the players with the hula hoops without getting one of the hula hoops placed over one's head. A player receives one point for each successful crossing. If a dribbler is "ringed" then he gives up his ball and takes the hula hoop. The player who has the most points wins.

MATERIALS: Balls, 3 hula hoops, a lined field or cones

AREA: This game may be played in a pre-marked area such as the 18 yard box or cones may be set out in a 40x20 area.

OBJECTIVE: Warm-up and liven the player's spirit, dribbling.

CHAIN TAG

HOW TO PLAY: This game starts out with 2-3 taggers. When the taggers "tag" one of the players then that player locks arms and becomes part of the chain. As players are tagged the chain(s) grow in size. The goal is once you are part of the chain to catch all the rest of the players who are not part of a chain.

MATERIALS: A lined field or cones.

AREA: This game may be played in a pre-marked area such as half of the 18 yard box or cones may be set out in a 30x30 area.

OBJECTIVE: Warm-up and liven the player's spirit.

KNEE TAG

HOW TO PLAY: In this game everyone plays against everyone. Players try to tag opponents on the knee without getting tagged on the knee themselves.

MATERIALS: A lined field or cones.

AREA: This game may be played in a pre-marked area such as half of the 18 yard box or cones may be set out in a 30x20 area.

STEAL THE BALL GAME

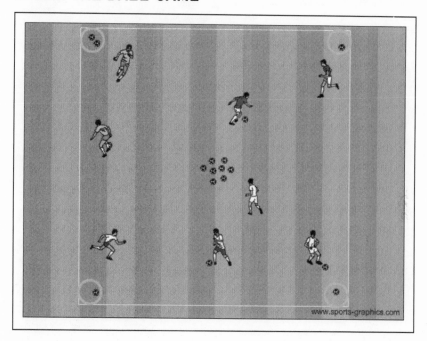

HOW TO PLAY: There are 4 teams each one starting out in a separate corner of a large square. One hula hoop is placed in each of the four corners of the area and they serve as scoring zones. A group of balls is placed in the very center of the square. On the word "go" the players from each team run to get a ball and dribble it back to their hula hoop. No hands are used in this game. Once all the balls are gone from the center, players may steal a ball from another team's hula hoop (only <u>one</u> at a time) or they may steal a ball from a player dribbling a ball. Nobody may guard their own goal.

MATERIALS: 4 hula hoops, cones, balls.

AREA: This game is played in a 30x30 square (field size should be adjusted to age/skill level of the players).

OBJECTIVE: Warm-up and liven the player's spirit, dribbling.

CUAUHTÉMOC GAME

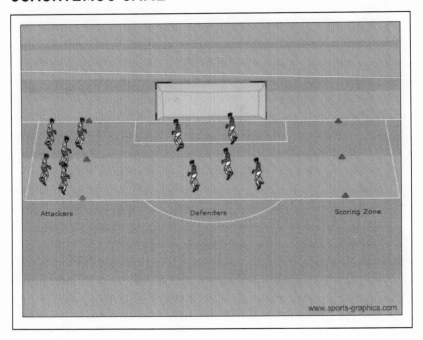

HOW TO PLAY: One team is attacking and the other defending. The attacking team tries to hop with the ball between their feet from one scoring zone all the way to the other scoring zone (other side of the 18 yard box). The defending team must also hop with a ball between their feet and try to knock the ball out of the attacker's feet. If the ball falls from the attacker's feet, then the attacker must go to the far scoring zone in order to begin another attempt to cross to the other side. Each successful crossing = 1 pt. Each team will have four tries to cross and then switch with the defending team. The team that finishes all four rounds with the most points wins.

MATERIALS: Cones, pinnies, balls.

AREA: This game may be played in a pre-marked area such as the entire 18 yard box or cones may be set out in a 40x20 area.

OBJECTIVE: Warm-up and liven the player's spirit, dribbling.

198

(1V2) DRIBBLING GAME

HOW TO PLAY: Form groups of three players. One player with the ball and two defending. Gain points by performing dribbling skill. Pass it off an opponent's leg and get it back = 1 point, nutmeg (through an opponent's legs and maintain possession) = 2 points, split the two opponents and maintain possession = 3 points.

MATERIALS: Cones, pinnies, balls.

AREA: This game may be played in a pre-marked area such as the entire 18 yard box or cones may be set out in a 30x30 area.

OBJECTIVE: Warm-up and liven the player's spirit, dribbling.

POSSESSION/HANDBALL

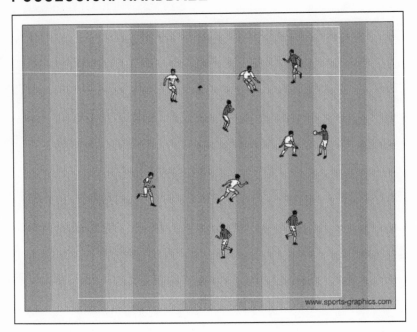

HOW TO PLAY: Form two teams of even numbers. There is one ball and the players must pass the ball with their hands. A team scores a point after making eight consecutive passes. If the ball drops or is intercepted there is a change of possession and the team with the ball starts counting again from zero. First team to score three points wins.

MATERIALS: cones, pinnies, balls.

AREA: This game can be played in half a field from the 18 yard box to the half-line – using the width of the 18 yard box as the other boundary.

OBJECTIVE: Warm-up and liven the player's spirit, perception, support of the ball

CONE TAG

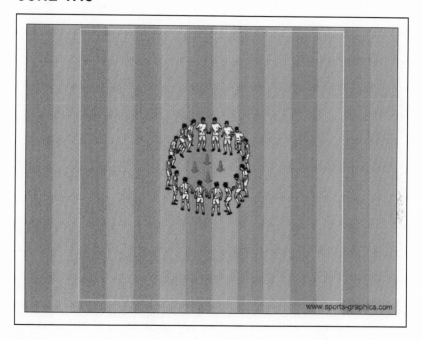

HOW TO PLAY: All players form a circle and hold hands. Players try to pull the opposite side of the circle in towards the cones in the middle. When a player touches a cone he becomes a tagger and must grab the cone and try to tag any of the other players before they leave the designated area. If the player with the cone is able to tag another player before leaving the area, that player will share the task. If the tagger cannot tag anyone then he will do the task alone. The task can be jumping jacks, bear crawls etc... If the circle breaks, the two players allowing the break are assigned a task. Pull the circle so that another member of the group touches a cone and becomes a tagger. Then escape the tagger so as to avoid doing the task.

MATERIALS: cones, pinnies, balls.

AREA: This game can be played in a square area of 35x35.

OBJECTIVE: Warm-up and liven the player's spirit.

(1V1) DRIBBLING GAME

HOW TO PLAY: Half the players with a ball and half without. The players with a ball dribble around the 18 yard box while the players without also move around without a ball. On the coaches' signal, the players play 1v1. The dribblers try to maintain possession while the opponents try to steal a ball and maintain possession themselves. Only one defender per attacker. If there is an extra player that person can join any of the other pairs to play 1v2. When the coach calls time the team with the most balls in their possession wins.

MATERIALS: pinnies, balls

AREA: This game can be played in the 18 yard box or a similar size area.

OBJECTIVE: Warm-up and liven the player's spirit, dribbling, winning the ball back/tackling.

RINGS GAME

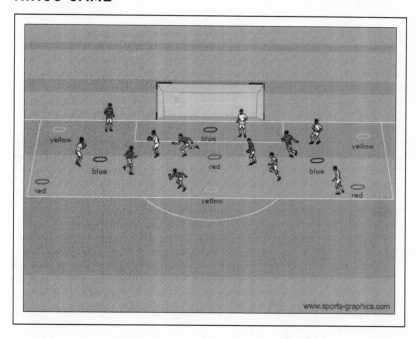

HOW TO PLAY: Three different sets of color rings (3 blue rings, 3 yellow rings and 3 red rings) are spread around the 18 yard box. There are two teams that pass the ball with their hands and try to score by placing the ball in one of the rings that is acting as a goal. Players with the ball only have two steps. The coach continually yells out a different color which changes where points can be scored. "yellow", "red", "blue" Pass the ball and score by placing the ball in one of the rings that is acting as a goal. First to three wins.

MATERIALS: rings, pinnies, balls. (I use Brazilian rubber balls)

AREA: This game can be played in the 18 yard box or an similar size area.

OBJECTIVE: Warm-up and liven the player's spirit, perception, support of the ball.

4 CONES GAME

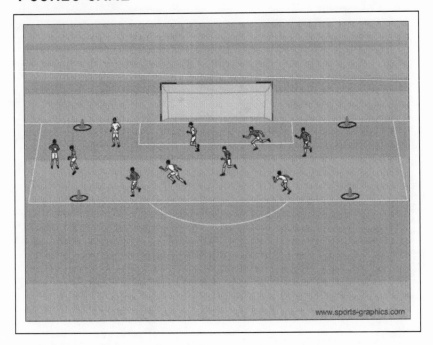

HOW TO PLAY: Four cones are placed within hula hoops spread out within the 18 yard box. There are two teams that each try to score by throwing the ball and knocking down any of the four cones. Pass the ball and score by knocking down a cone. First to three wins.

MATERIALS: hula hoops, cones, pinnies, balls. (I use Brazilian rubber balls) *see chapter on equipment.

AREA: This game can be played in the 18 yard box or a similar sized area.

OBJECTIVE: Warm-up and liven the player's spirit, perception, support of the ball.

CHAPTER 20

Rondos, Possession Games, and Positional Games

"Everything that goes on in a match, except shooting, you can do in a rondo. The competitive aspect, fighting to make space, what to do when in possession and what to do when you haven't got the ball, how to play one touch soccer, how to counteract the tight marking and how to win the ball back."

Johan Cruijff (Legendary player for F.C. Barcelona and Holland)

Definition of "rondo": A game where one group of players has the ball while in numerical superiority (3v1, 5v2, 5v5+2 etc...) over another group of players. The basic objective of the group in numerical superiority is to keep possession of the ball while the objective of the group in numerical inferiority is to win the ball back. Rondos differ from other possession games in that the rondo is a game where the players occupy a preset space as opposed to a more random space. Positional games are games where players occupy spaces similar to those in the regular game e.g., outside back, center back, center midfield etc... On the following pages are a few of the variations of rondos and positional games.

Rondos help develop the following areas:

(Article: <u>El juego del rondo y su aplicación práctica al entrenamiento de equipos de fútbol de alto rendimiento</u> - Alberto Martín Barrero and Francisco Ignacio Martínez Cabrera – Faculty of Sport: Pablo de Olavide University, Spain)

COGNITIVE. In rondos the player is constantly perceiving and making decisions with respect to his teammates, opponents, position of the ball etc… For this reason the capacity to make the correct decisions and the speed of play are improved.

TECHNICAL COORDINATION. Due to the way that the rondo is set up, it is necessary to have control of the physical movements and technical skills with respect to time and space, the game, the ball and opponents.

TEAM BUILDING. (mini societies) With the type of work done in rondos, the understanding between teammates is improved, and the sense of "team" is also built.

CREATIVITY AND EXPRESSION. The nature of the rondo, with its limited time and space, forces the players to use various technical and tactical abilities in order to solve constantly changing problems within the game. This helps develop creativity.

COMPETITIVENESS. In the development of the rondo, the player's competitive nature is improved. Players have to fight to make space, learn how to counteract marking and how to win the ball back. Nobody wants to be the one making the mistake which leads to time in the middle.

PHYSICAL CONDITIONING. With rondos a team may work anaerobic resistance by varying the space, time and number of players involved.

Rondo - 5v2/6v2/7v2

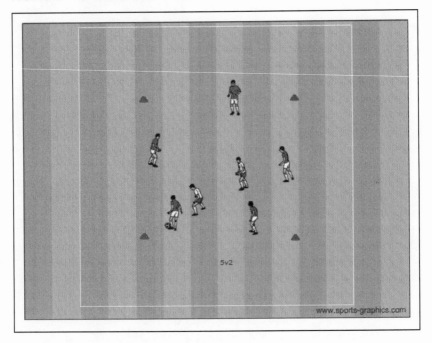

HOW TO PLAY: In this activity there is one team of 5-7 players within a 10 by 10 yard grid. Another two players are in the middle trying to win the ball back. They should hold a pinnie in one hand. Players in possession (depending on the level) are limited to one touch or two touches. When a player in possession makes a mistake and possession is lost, the player making the mistake must switch places with one of the players in the middle. If the ball goes out of play it should be put back in play quickly from a kick in from the ground. Extra balls should be placed around the outside of the area to help maintain the flow of the game.

Rondo - 6v2 mini square

HOW TO PLAY: In this activity there is one team of 6-7 players within a 15 yard grid that tries to maintain possession. There are two players in the middle trying to win the ball back. They each hold a pinnie in one hand. Players in possession (depending on the level) are limited to one touch or two touches. There is also a smaller 5 yard grid in the middle of the larger grid. Each time the team in possession is able to pass the ball through the smaller grid and maintain possession, it earns a point. If a player in the middle wins the ball back he switches places with the attacker that made the mistake. Restarts from a kick in. The team with the most points after a set time period wins. Extra balls should be placed around the outside of the area to help maintain the flow of the game.

Rondo - 4v4+3 Neutrals

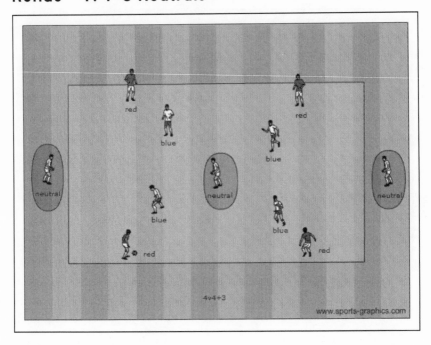

HOW TO PLAY: In this activity there are two teams of four players with three neutrals: one in the middle and two outside the area. Neutrals support the team in possession. Each time a team is able to go (passing the ball) from one of the neutrals on one side to the other neutral on the other side they earn a point. When a team loses possession all their players must transition quickly to win the ball back. The team that wins possession passes the ball to a neutral and then opens up on the outside. The transition is done as quickly as possible. The team with the most points after a set time period wins. Extra balls should be placed next to one of the neutrals on the outside of the area to help maintain the flow of the game. Restarts always from one of the neutrals. High tempo game for short periods. Three rounds of 4-5 minutes each.

Rondo - 5v5+2 Neutrals

HOW TO PLAY: In this activity there are two teams of five players with two neutrals in wide areas. Neutrals support the team in possession. Each time a team is able to have one neutral touch the ball and then, after a sequence of passes, the other neutral touches the ball, a point is earned. Upon winning the ball back a team must play to one of the neutral players to continue play. This team then spreads out with 4 of 5 players finding spaces on the outside of the area. When a team loses possession they must transition quickly to the middle attempting to win the ball back. The team with the most points after a set time period wins. Extra balls should be placed next to one of the neutrals on the outside of the area to help maintain the flow of the game. Restarts always from one of the neutrals. High intensity game with quick transitions. Three rounds of 4-5 minutes each.

Rondo with transition - 5v2 in two zones

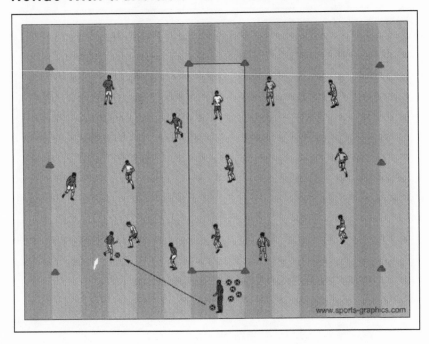

HOW TO PLAY: In this activity there are three teams of 5 players with two teams maintaining possession and one team in the middle trying to win the ball back. The coach starts with the ball and passes to one of the two teams in the wide grids. Two defenders may go try to win the ball back while another thee remain in the central "interception" zone. The team in possession must make four passes in their zone before trying to play across to the other side. Each time a team in possession is successful in making four passes and then a pass across to the other zone they get a point. Each team spends 5 minutes defending in the middle. The object is to be the team that has accumulated the most points at the end of the 15 minutes. High intensity game.

3 Rondos with Transition

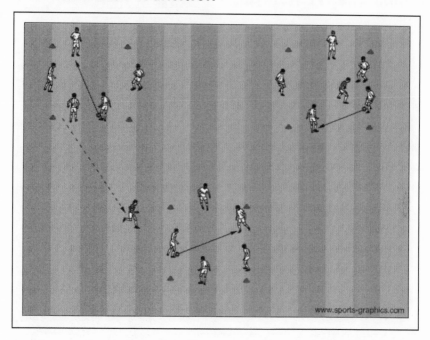

HOW TO PLAY: In this activity there are three groups of five players possessing the ball one touch. (3 ten yard boxes) Two players (one each in two of the three boxes) begin as defenders and whenever possession is lost, the player making the mistake becomes a defender. This defender must leave the box he is in and find (sprinting) another grid where there are no defenders. There will always be one box open with no defender. The cycle continues. A group with no defender still must keep the ball moving 1 touch and must be aware of the arrival of the next defender. Extra balls should be placed around the outside of each box to keep the flow of the game going. Progression: after a pass get around a cone in your grid. (pass and move)

Rondo - 3v3+2 Neutrals

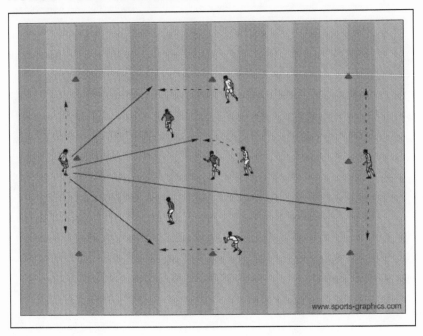

HOW TO PLAY: In this activity there are two teams of three players in the middle zone and two neutral players acting as support on the outside. The objective is to maintain possession and pass the ball from one side to the other to the neutral players. Each time a team in possession is able to complete a set number of passes, they receive a point. The team with the most points wins after a set amount of time wins. When possession is lost, the ball is passed to a neutral player and the players on the outside collapse and try to win the ball back. The players who were defending now open to the outside and possess the ball. Restarts from kick ins. Extra balls should be placed around the outside of the area to help maintain the flow of the game. Three rounds of 4-5 minutes.

Possession game - 8v6 with transition

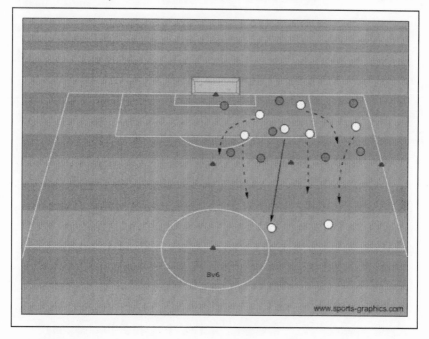

HOW TO PLAY: There are two teams of eight players in one quarter of a field. The area is split into two zones. One team maintains possession while the other team tries to win the ball back. The defending team must leave two players in the opposite zone. When they win the ball back, they must pass the ball to one of the two players in the opposite zone and transition to that zone where they will attempt to maintain possession. A team scores a point after making 7 consecutive passes. Restarts are from a kick in. Extra balls should be placed around the outside of the area to help maintain the flow of the game.

OBJECTIVE: *To improve possession, passing and transition.

MATERIALS: cones, pinnies, balls.

AREA: One quarter of the field split into two zones.

Possession game with transition - 3v3+3, 4v4+4 or 5v5+5

HOW TO PLAY: There are three teams of (3, 4 or 5) players. Two of the teams possess the ball and the third team tries to win it back. When the team in the middle wins the ball back, the team in possession that made the mistake transitions back to the middle as defenders. Play lasts for two 8 minute periods. Restarts are from a kick in. Extra balls should be placed around the outside of the area to help maintain the flow of the game.

OBJECTIVE: *To improve possession and moments of transition.

MATERIALS: cones, pinnies, balls

AREA: Should be adjusted to the number and level of players involved. (3v3+3 – 35x25, 4v4+4 – 45x35, and 5v5+5 - 55x45)

Possession game – 8v8 to diagonal support

HOW TO PLAY: An area is marked out from the width of the 18 yard box to the half line with a gate on each corner. There are two teams of equal numbers with one member of each team (support players) located diagonally on each corner gate. There is one ball in play. When a pass is made to a support player, someone from the field must take the target player's place. A point is scored each time a team connects with a player stationed at one of the diagonal corners and maintains possession. A team may not go back to the same corner until they have made four passes. The object is to try to connect with the support player at the far diagonal corner and to score points by maintaining possession. Play for a set amount of time. The team with the most amount of points at the end of time wins.

OBJECTIVE: *To improve possession, support play, passing, switching the point of attack and finding numerical superiority.

MATERIALS: cones, pinnies, balls.

AREA: Between the 18 yd. box and the half-line. The width of the 18 yd box.

Positional Game - 2v2+2 Neutrals

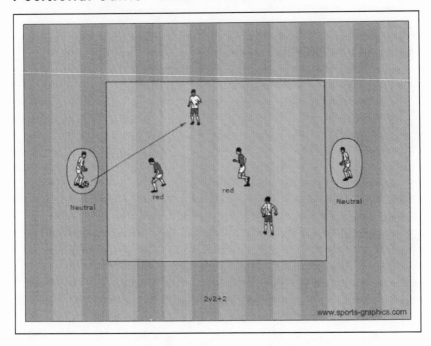

HOW TO PLAY: In this activity there are two teams of two players with the support of two neutrals playing in a rectangular space. The neutrals take up the position of the center back and a forward just outside the area. Neutrals may not make more than two passes directly between each other. A point is scored each time the ball is touched by one neutral and then through a sequence of passes ends with the other neutral. If both players in the middle touch the ball before passing to the opposite neutral it counts as two points. The team with the most points after a set time period wins. Restarts are from a kick in from a neutral. High intensity game. Play 5 minutes and change the neutrals. Three rounds of 5 minutes each.

Positional Game – 4v4+4 Neutrals

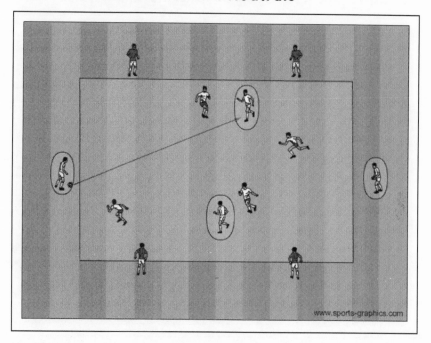

HOW TO PLAY: In this activity there are two teams of four players with the support of four neutrals playing in a rectangular space. There are two neutrals inside the area and two neutrals outside the area. Neutrals may not make more than two passes directly between each other. A point is scored each time the ball is touched by one neutral and then through a sequence of passes ends with the other neutral. If both players in the middle touch the ball before passing to the opposite neutral it counts as two points. The team with the most points after a set time period wins. Restarts are from a kick in from a neutral. High intensity game. Play 5 minutes and change the neutrals. Three rounds of 5 minutes each.

Positional Game - 6v6+2 Neutrals

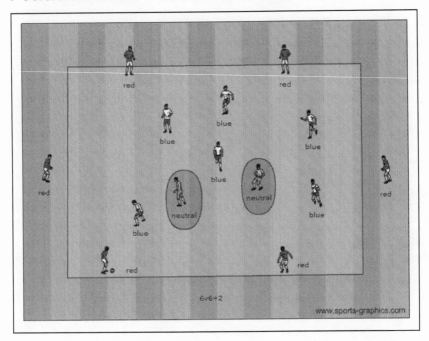

HOW TO PLAY: In this activity there are two teams of six players with two neutrals in the middle. Each time a team is able to complete a set number of passes, they earn a point. When the team on the outside loses possession all of their players must transition to winning the ball back by collapsing and closing the ball in the middle. If the ball goes out of play it is put back in play by the team in possession with the coach passing to one of the neutrals. The team with the most points in a set amount of time wins. The coach must have a supply of balls in order to help maintain the flow of the game. High intensity game. Play 5 minutes and change the neutrals. Three rounds of 5 minutes each.

Positional Game - 5v5+6 Neutrals

HOW TO PLAY: In this activity there are six neutral players - a goalkeeper, two center backs, two outside backs and a forward outside the central grid (4-3-3 in logical game positions). Ten players with five on each team are located in the central grid. The sequence always starts from the goalkeeper playing out to a center back. The objective is to play out from the back through the midfield and arrive to the forward. <u>Two touch restriction</u>. Each time possession is lost, the ball starts again from the keeper. In order to score, the ball must be passed from a midfield player to the forward. Progression: One player trying to win the ball back may leave the central grid.

Positional Game - 6v2+1 Neutral to goal

HOW TO PLAY: This activity is played in two different adjoining grids with transition to goal. There are 6 players from team A in one grid and 6 players from team B in an adjoining grid. Each team also has one player (winger) stationed in a wide position. The play starts with a service from the coach. Two opponents cross into the opposite grid to try and win the ball back. If they win the ball back, they play across to their teammates. After the team in possession makes three passes within the grid, the ball is played to the winger and one more attacker from inside the grid overlaps in order to create a 2v1 to goal. The wide pass must go outside the central space designated by the two poles. One defender from the opposite grid can go and defend. The first team to score three goals wins. <u>Progression:</u> allow more attackers to attack the goal and more defenders to defend. The coach should demand quick transition after change of possession.

🌎 Young professional players during a game in Rio de Janeiro, Brazil.

CHAPTER 21

Perception

"Simplified games should frequently be played to four small goals rather than to just two. This will help players improve their decision making and perception." – Horst Wein (Author and internationally renowned coaching mentor.)

The important role that perception plays in the development of youth soccer players cannot be understated. By definition, perception means "the act or faculty of apprehending by means of the senses or of the mind; cognition; understanding." When Horst Wein states that "soccer is a game that begins in the head, flows through the heart, and ends in the feet." he is pointing out that every action on the field begins with a player perceiving his environment, processing that picture visually, and making a decision based on the visual snapshot through a process in the brain. In other words, the entire decision making process starts with what a player is able to see happening in the game.

Since eighty five percent of the information a player processes comes from his eyes, it is extremely important to train this part of our overall sensory perception. A player can only perform an action as well as he can process what he sees correctly, and seeing the correct things is a skill anyone can learn to improve. The eyes of a player can only see and recognize what the brain knows, and the more a player knows, the more experienced he becomes, and the more the player is able to see, to detect or to read from a game situation on the field.

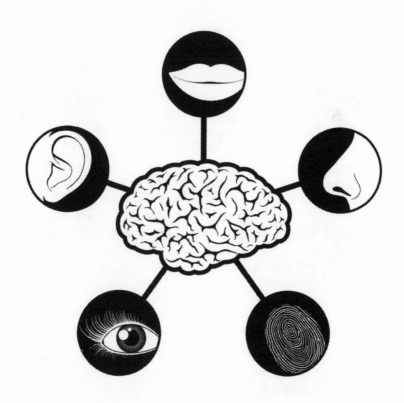

In order to understand why perception is so important in soccer, and how it relates to soccer specific skill, it is important to recognize that soccer is considered an open or complex sport. Open sports are those such as ice hockey, tennis and basketball where the environment has constantly changing variables. In comparison, a closed sport such as gymnastics, does not have such an environment where performance is affected by outside variables. The skills needed for a sport such as gymnastics take place in a stable, non- fluctuating environment and the skills are habitual. On the other hand, due to the constantly changing nature of its environment, the skills for soccer are predominantly perceptual. As the game progresses, the placement on the field of opponents, teammates and the ball is constantly changing. Each player takes thousands of visual pictures during a game, that when processed by the brain, lead to decisions that can positively or negatively influence the outcome of the game for his team. The more a player sees and is able to process, the clearer the understanding will be of what the player should do next.

"Players lose possession of many balls or they complicate the play by not observing, before receiving the ball, the position of teammates and opponents."
– Alejandro Scopelli (Argentine author, coach, and World Cup player)

There are many visual stimulants present in the game of soccer. These include the player with the ball, the situation and placement of teammates, the situation and placement of the opponents, the distance between teammates and opponents, and the zone of the field where the action is taking place. Faced with numerous stimulants, a player must manage each situation selecting the appropriate solution.

Often the only difference between an average player and an outstanding player is the skill of perception. Players such as Xavi and Iniesta at Barcelona are masters of seeing what is around them and then making decisions based on what the game is telling them they should do next. These players always appear calm and composed when under pressure in a game. A major reason for this composure comes from their highly developed sense of perception and peripheral vision which helps them anticipate what will happen next in the game. Of course both players have also developed a high level of decision making and technical ability which allows them to choose the correct play and to execute it successfully. Just as decision making and technique can be improved through proper training, a player's perception can also be improved.

As coaches, we should be continuously searching out ways to help our players improve their game. The frequent use of visual skill training not only helps a player to track the ball and opponents as well as team-mates more quickly and accurately, it will vastly improve peripheral awareness, reaction time, capacity of anticipation and, most importantly, the ability to maintain mental focus for an entire game.

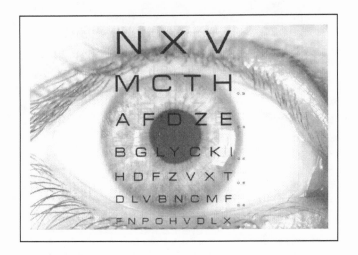

Training perception by limiting vision

Diego Armando Maradona, in the documentary "Maradona" by Kusturica, speaks about how he and his friends loved to play so much that they would continue playing even after the sun went down. He mentions how they would play a lot at night in situations where it was very difficult to see the ball, teammates, the opponents, or the goal. According to Maradona, playing with a vision handicap at night brought out a higher sensitivity of perception when playing in the daytime. He points out how he could truly see a difference and that his overall play improved dramatically in the daytime after struggling to perceive the environment at night. One way to limit vision and to handicap depth perception during training sessions is to use either goggles or an eye patch over one of the player's eyes. Frequently taking away a player's peripheral vision and depth perception will help heighten sensitivity to this form of perception and in turn will make it easier to perceive the ball, opponents, teammates, and the goal when taking away the handicap. Note: this should not be done until around 14-15 years old. (Laureano Ruiz) On the following pages I have included some activities to help improve a soccer player's perception.

 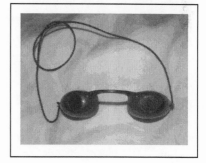

☆ Eye patch and goggles.

Perception Passing

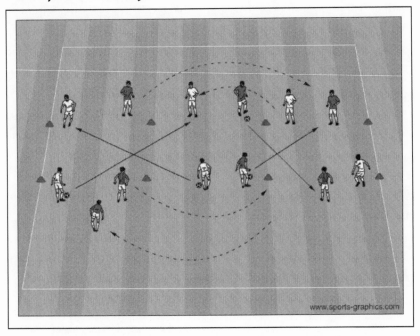

www.sports-graphics.com

1. Form two teams of different colored pinnies and create a <u>7-10 yard channel</u> 40 yards long across the width of the field.

2. Players pass the ball <u>one touch on the ground</u> in partners. They must stay outside the channel. ✪ (Only ask the players to play one touch if they are ready technically.)

3. Players pass the ball <u>one touch</u> and move forwards and backwards.

4. Players pass the ball <u>two touch</u>. ✪ (Players should pass the ball hard to their teammate's feet and always on the ground. This will allow for practice of the first touch. Ask players to take first touch away from pressure.)

5. Organize players with half of each team (red) on each side of the channel.

6. Players play <u>two touch</u> (diagonal passes only) to a teammate and then move to a supporting position to receive a pass from a different teammate.

7. Players play <u>two touch</u> (diagonal passes only) and then move to the opposite side of the channel with a change of speed.

Perception Passing (with turns)

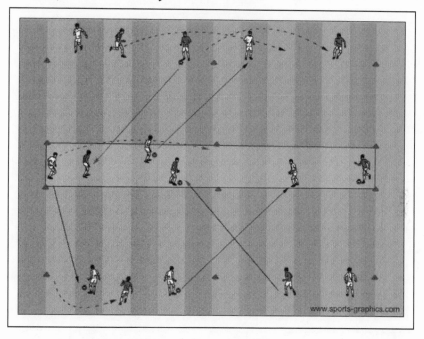

★ Form two teams of (8-9) players wearing different colored pinnies and create a <u>7-10 yard channel</u> 40 yards long across the width of the field. Have 2-3 players from each team on each end and in the central zone. The players in the middle will work on getting a good sideways position to receive and turn. Start with two balls for each team.

Key: All passes must be diagonal, with lots of speed to feet. All players on the outer zones have two touches, and players in the middle are encouraged to take two touches (one to receive and one to pass) although they may take a third touch to create a better passing angle. Once a pass is made, all players are encouraged to move away to find another space.

3 Team Passing

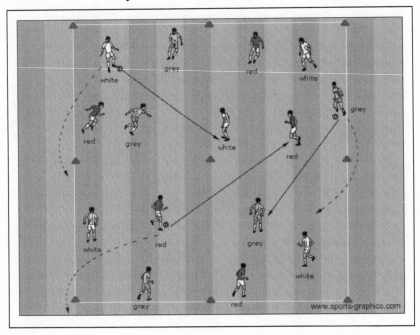

1. Form three teams with different colored pinnies.

2. In a 35 x 35 area, players pass the ball to anyone else (hands) and then move away.

3. Players pass the ball to anyone else (feet) and then move away.

4. Players pass the ball to a teammate (feet) and then move away.

5. Players pass the ball (feet) to a teammate and then move around an outside cone with a change of speed.

6. Players pass the ball to a teammate (feet), move around a cone with a change of speed. Now the pass must be to a teammate in another quadrant.

7. Players pass the ball to a teammate (feet) in another quadrant, get it back, and play to someone else. At the end of the sequence the player who passes the ball moves around an outside cone with a chance of speed.

8. Players pass the ball in a sequence of color (feet). (Example: red, orange, yellow) Red team passes to orange, orange to yellow, and yellow back to red. After a pass the player must move around an outside cone with a change of speed.

Coaching Points: communication, movement after the pass, movement towards the ball, first touch, speed of the pass, support angles.

Perception with dribblers

⭐ In a rectangular area 40x25 there are three teams of 5 players each. Four players from each team are inside the area and 1 from each team is outside the area dribbling a ball (They should try to maintain an even distance from each other). Players inside the area must constantly observe which players are dribbling in the narrow zones outside the rectangle. The players inside the area pass the ball with a two touch maximum. They have to pass to a player who is of the same color as the player or players dribbling in the narrow zones. In this case of the graphic above, the red player with the ball (circle) can pass to a player who is either red or blue. This is the case since at the moment he receives a pass a red and a blue dribbler are both in the narrow zones at the same time. If there is only one dribbler in a narrow zone (example: blue) the next pass must go to a blue player. If no players are in the narrow zone then the player with the ball has the option of passing to any color. Every so often switch dribblers.

Perception with different colored balls

★ This <u>6v6 game</u> is played with three balls in a <u>45 x 35 area</u>. One ball is played on the ground with feet and two balls of different colors are passed by the hands. (one colored ball each team) Players holding a colored ball may not attack nor defend. They cannot become active again until they pass the ball to someone else. Other players must be aware of which players are holding a different colored ball. A team cannot score if their colored ball drops and is on the ground. They can only be eligible to score again once the ball is being held in the hands. First to a set number of goals wins.

3v3+3 Faces

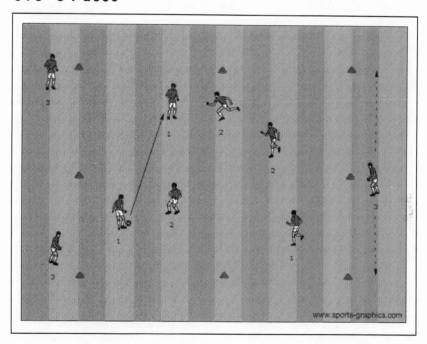

☆ In this perception game, played in a <u>25x35 area</u> instead of focusing on passing to a specific color, the focus transfers to looking for faces. Three teams of three players play a possession game, and each team is given a number 1, 2 or 3. Players may pass to members of the same team plus the other team in possession (6v3). One team of three takes up a position on the outside with two corner support players on one side, and one player on the other side who can move up and down the line. The players on the outside have one touch. All players wear the same color pinnie.

<u>Progression:</u> A player cannot give the ball back to the teammate who passed it to him.

Numbers Passing with traffic

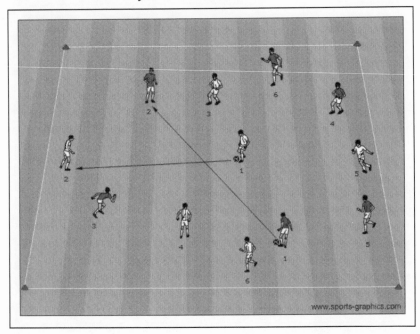

★ In this game there are various groups of players passing the ball in the same approximate area. Within each team, the ball must go in sequence from 1 to 2, 2 to 3, etc... When it gets to the player with the highest number it goes back to one again. The players' perception is challenged due to the substantial movement and different color pinnies within the same area.

Progressions: The restriction starts with two touches and then reduces to one touch. Once the players have good control of passing with one ball they should then add a second ball.

Moveable Goals Game

⭐ In this game two teams compete by trying to score on moveable goals. Two players from each team hold a pole on their shoulders and move around constantly within the area of play. They try to make it difficult for the opposing team to score, but they may not leave the area. The first team to score three goals wins. Players are challenged in that they need to constantly scan the field to see where the goal they are attacking is located. *Use PVC piping to make two poles for the goals.

"Chaotic" Games in One Area (4 Goals)

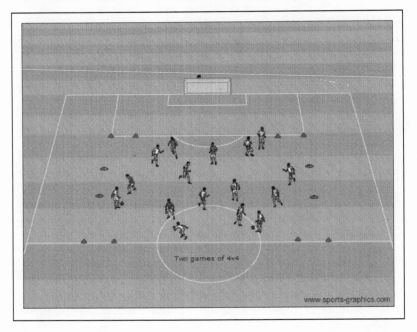

☆ In this game there are two separate 4v4 games (With four 2-yard wide goals) going on within the same area. (Edge of the 18 yard box to half field) Each team attacks and defends two goals. If the ball goes out of play it is restarted with a kick in. Two 7 minute games. Rotate the teams playing against each other. This game is great for challenging the player's perception.

* For more exercises for training perception, see chapter on small sided games: <u>Horst Wein's Mini Soccer with 4 goals</u>)

🌐 A Brazilian Confederation van at the CBF Training Center.

Each action in soccer

1 STARTS IN THE HEAD

2 FLOWS THROUGH THE HEART

3 AND ENDS IN THE FEET

Horst Wein

CHAPTER 22

Decision Making and Game Intelligence

"The fastest player is not the one who runs the fastest yet the one who solves the game's problems the fastest." – <u>Cesar Luis Menotti</u> (Coach of World Champion – Argentina 1978)

Along with perception and technique, game intelligence is a critical part of a player's development in the game of soccer. Laureano Ruiz, former coach at F.C Barcelona, points out in his book <u>Soccer: Secrets of Success</u>, how great athletes or even players who are highly skilled technically, do not automatically translate into great soccer players. In his opinion, the characteristic that sets a true soccer player apart when compared to athletes from other sports is game intelligence. He states "Many players have the ability to run, jump, control the ball and shoot very well, but they don't know how to play the game. Soccer skills are difficult to master but they are simple when compared to the infinite combination of things a player can be faced with on the pitch, but it is essential for a player to master this knowledge if he is to achieve his full potential". Gaining the necessary soccer intelligence takes years of practice during which time players are put in situations where they must perceive, analyze and execute as the situation around them constantly changes.

"Our aim to is to help young players understand the game. Of course, there is the emphasis on technique, where it all starts. But we want the players to learn how to think fast. We want them to learn how to run little, but run smart." – Pep Guardiola

In many countries throughout the world, the emphasis is heavily weighted toward analytical technical training so decision making in global simplified games is sometimes forgotten. This is a huge mistake. According to Horst Wein, in an interview with ESPN in Argentina, the statistics point to the fact that at the professional level, more than fifty percent of the time, loss of possession is due to an error in decision making and not at all related to an error in technique. This points to how important it is to develop game intelligence and its relation to a team's ability to maintain possession.

So how should a modern coach go about developing game intelligence? According to Horst Wein, the three primary areas of a coaching style that place emphasis on the development of game intelligence are:

1. A player-centered, active-learning coaching style
2. Games rather than drills
3. Effective open ended questioning

One of the most knowledgeable and experienced coaching leaders in the United States, Manny Schellscheidt, states that "the best players are the ones who are able to process multiple bits of information that are flowing from the game." Schellscheidt, who most recently was in charge of the United States U14 boy's national team, believes the mental side of the game is extremely important. In his training sessions, mental preparation is emphasized just as much as technical ability. He states "The great players lead with their minds. They ask themselves questions such as "How do I make space and time? How do I take it away?"

🌐 Mini - goals for small-sided games at Club Atlético Independiente's training grounds – Buenos Aires, Argentina. The place where many great players have trained including <u>Sergio "Kun" Ague ro</u> and <u>Diego Forlan</u>.

CHAPTER 23

Small-Sided/Global Games

"Very much of what my father did in practice replicated the street soccer he grew up with in the streets of Argentina. And street soccer usually meant small-sided games. In a small space, players have to make quick decisions on the ball and be able to handle it under pressure, because an opponent is usually close by." – Claudio Reyna.

As youth soccer has evolved around the world, it has become more widely recognized that it is a mistake to train young players as if they were adults. It is essential that our youngsters are presented with a simplified game format to match their physical, cognitive and technical abilities. So how do smaller numbers of players and a smaller field correlate to better soccer development? In a recent study (2002-2003) focusing on U9 boys playing in the Youth Academy at Manchester United Football Club in England, data was collected by Dr. Rick Fenoglio, a lecturer in Exercise Science at Manchester Metropolitan University. In the study, a series of fifteen 4v4 and 8v8 games were videotaped and analyzed. The following chart shows the findings of the data. The results do not lie. From the data it is clear that the smaller number of players bring about a higher level of involvement in the game. Players have a more difficult time hiding in a 4v4 game than an 8v8 or 11v11 game.

Evidence for smaller numbers.

(Manchester United Youth Academy: Study of 4v4 vs 8v8 games - U9 Boys)

PASSES	+135% or 585 more passes in 4v4 games than in 8v8 games
SHOTS TAKEN	+260% or 481 more shots in 4v4 games than in 8v8 games
GOALS SCORED	+500% or 301 more goals in 4v4 games than in 8v8 games
1V1'S	+225% or 525 more 1v1's in 4v4 games than in 8v8 games
TRICKS, TURNS, MOVES	+280% or 436 more tricks, turns, and moves than in 8v8 games

In an 11v11 game the average player has approximately 90 seconds to two minutes of contact with the ball. This is simply not enough to develop players to a higher level. As we can see in the following chart, if players are exposed to a higher number of properly run training sessions where they are exposed to small-sided games, the panorama changes dramatically. A player's average contact with the ball goes from 90 seconds to upwards of 20 minutes per training session.

CONTACT WITH THE BALL IN AN AVERAGE TRAINING SESSION

Activity	Ratio of players to one ball	Time participating in minutes	Time that the activity involves a ball	Average time contacting the ball
Warm-up	6:1	15	100%	2.5 min
individual analytical technique + 3v3	1:1, 3:1	15	100%	7.5 min
2v2	4:1	20	100%	5 min
4v4	8:1	30	100%	3.75
6v6, 8v8, 11v11	12:1, 16:1, 22:1	30	100%	2.5

★ Total average time a player is in contact with the ball in a training session = <u>over 20 minutes compared to between 90-120 seconds in an 11v11 game</u>.[25]

[25] Chart: LA IMPORTANCIA DEL JUEGO EN ESPACIOS REDUCIDOS
Óscar Méndez Albano http://www.desdeadentrodelvestuario.blogspot.com 2009.

A great foundation for player development using simplified games is found in Horst Wein's Mini - Soccer game (Now referred to as Funiño) with scoring zones. The dimensions are 32 yards long by 20 yards wide. There are two scoring zones of 6 yards each. Goals are 2 yards wide and are placed in wide areas. The game is played in various ways with beginners playing 3v0, then 3v1, 3v2 and finally 3v3. The key is to have players progress to a more complex game only when they are ready. The measurements in the diagram on the following page are set up for a 3v3 game, but the field can be adjusted depending on the age and number of players.

According to Wein, playing to four wide goals with an odd number of players (3v3, 5v5, 7v7) is more beneficial to player development than to two central goals since players must constantly perceive and then make decisions based on where the attackers can gain numerical superiority. (They must quickly decide which goal is less defended.) Another reason this format is so powerful is that there are infinite variations of how the game can be played; thus, allowing for different challenges for the players and higher motivation. Another huge benefit is that the game is integral in nature. This means that within the game the players learn perception, decision making and technique all at the same time.

HORST WEIN'S MINI-SOCCER (FUNIÑO)

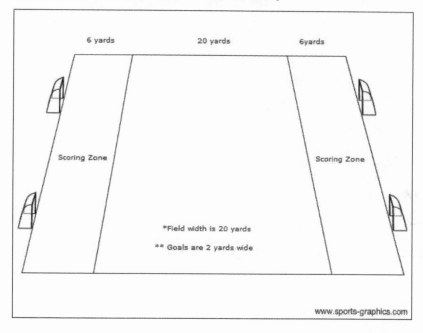

6 yards   20 yards   6yards

Scoring Zone   Scoring Zone

*Field width is 20 yards

** Goals are 2 yards wide

www.sports-graphics.com

Horst Wein's mini soccer field for 3v3. Field dimensions are 20 yards. by 32 yards long with two 6 yard scoring zones at each end. The four goals are stationed in the wide areas of the end line and are two yards in width.

SOME OF THE BENEFITS OF MINI SOCCER TO 4 GOALS.

1. More touches on the ball.

2. More opportunity for overall skill development.

3. More attacking opportunities.

4. More defending opportunities.

5. Helps improve perception and awareness.

6. More opportunities to solve the games problems.

7. Nobody can hide when on the field. Everyone is involved.

8. Encourages faster play and quicker thinking.

9. More scoring opportunities and more goals scored.

10. More fun to play!

20 VARIATIONS OF HORST WEIN'S MINI-SOCCER.

1. All members of a team must touch the ball before scoring.

2. The ball cannot be lifted off the ground or it is considered a turnover.

3. When a goal is scored, all attacking players must be over the halfway line.

4. One player must stay in depth at the back in the other team's scoring zone.

5. One player must stay forward in the scoring zone giving depth in attack.

6. The forward in the scoring zone is the only player who can't score.

7. If you score you keep the ball and attack in the opposite direction.

8. A goal may only be scored from the central zone.

9. The ball must be dribbled through the goal in order to score.

10. Two touch limit in defensive half/unlimited in attacking half

11. (3,2,1) – Each time your team scores your team gets one less touch. (Start with three touches each team and go down to one touch. Reset back to three touches after playing 1 touch.)

12. Players alternate 1 then 2 touch. (First player = 1 touch, second player = 2 touches, third player back to = 1 touch etc…)

13. Only touch the ball with the weaker foot. (Have players pull their sock down.)

14. Play with goalkeepers who must move between the two goals.

15. A 2v1 (overlap) must occur before a team can score.

16. The ball must be in the air as it enters the goal.

17. Attack and defend diagonal goals. (Defend our right goal and attack the opponent's left goal)

18. Each team only has 7 touches maximum and then they must shoot.

19. First goal dribbling, second goal passing and third goal with the head.

20. Goals must be scored on a preset trick. Example: Back-heel.

🌐 Argentina Subbuteo player[26]

"I go about the world, hand outstretched, and in the stadiums I plead: A pretty move, for the love of God. And when good soccer happens, I give thanks for the miracle and I don't give a damn which team or country performs it." – Eduardo Galeano (Uruguayan author of Fútbol en Sol y Sombra)

---

[26] Photograph: Inkwina - Wikimedia Commons 2007.

1, 2, 3 GAME

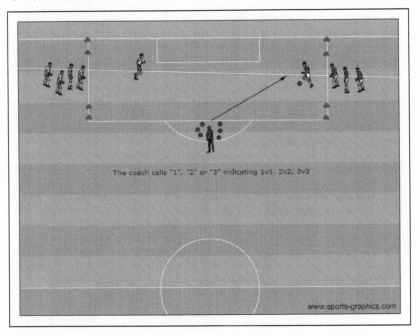

The coach calls "1", "2" or "3" indicating 1v1, 2v2, 3v3

www.sports-graphics.com

HOW TO PLAY: In this game there are two teams with different color pinnies who each are stationed at the edge of the width of the 18 yard box. There are four small goals with two on each end of the area. The coach is stationed in the D and serves balls in and calls a number "1", "2", or "3". The number called refers to how many players come on to the field to play for each team. The service should be continuous from the coach and there should be multiple games going on at the same time. Players attack two goals and defend two goals. The team that is the first to score ten goals wins.

OBJECTIVE: *To improve 1v1 duels and decision making in small numbers.

MATERIALS: cones, pinnies, balls

AREA: The area within the 18 yard box.

2 Boxes Game (dribbling 1v1 and 1v2)

HOW TO PLAY: In this game players are in partners and play 1v1. One player starts with the ball and attempts to score by dribbling in and out of one of the boxes. If he is successful he must try to attack the other box. If the defender wins possession he immediately becomes the attacker. Play for 45 seconds to 1 minute and then rest. Play 6 rounds with different partners.

OBJECTIVE: *To improve 1v1 duels and decision making in small numbers.

MATERIALS: cones, pinnies, balls

AREA: The area between the half line and the 18 yard box. Two 10x10 scoring boxes.

PROGRESSION: Form groups of three with one dribbler and two defenders.

2v2 (2 touch)

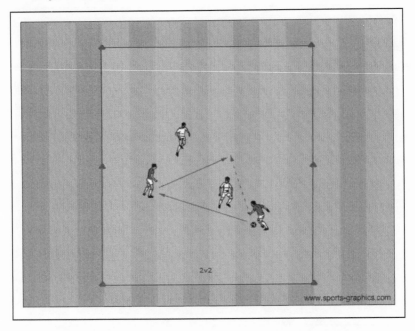

HOW TO PLAY: I observed this game at Botafogo Futebol Clube in Rio de Janeiro, Brazil. Players must learn to quickly move to a supporting position after passing the ball. Since there are only two touches, players also learn how to let the ball run "invisible control" without taking unnecessary touches. They also learn to be creative in combining with their teammate. (outside of the foot, backheels, flicks etc...) To score, a player must stop the ball on the other side of the opposite end line. (15x20 yards)

OBJECTIVE: *To improve <u>combination play</u>, <u>quick thinking</u> and <u>off the ball movement</u>.

MATERIALS: cones, pinnies (optional), balls

AREA: 20 x25 yards

Brazilian Keep Away (Bobinho)

Brazilian Triangle Game 3v1

www.sports-graphics.com

HOW TO PLAY: Brazilian keep away is called "Bobinho" This (3v1) is played with one ball, three attackers and one defender. The defender can move along the lines of the triangle but cannot go out and get the ball from the players in possession. A point is scored every time the ball is successfully played through the triangle on the ground maintaining possession. If possession is lost, the player making the mistake takes the place of the defender in the middle.

"He who can play 3 v 3 successfully can play soccer!"
— Cesar Luis Menotti (Coach of Argentina 1978)

Heading/volleying Game

HOW TO PLAY: Form two teams of even numbers. There is one ball and the players must pass the ball with their hands. After catching a ball, a player may move only two steps before passing the ball to a teammate. If the ball drops to the ground there is a change of possession. A 3 yard goal is placed on each end of the playing area. Goals must be scored on a header. The first team to score three goals wins.

OBJECTIVE: *To improve heading and volleying technique along with support play and movement off the ball.

MATERIALS: cones, pinnies, balls, poles.

VARIATION: Volley Game - This game may also be played with the players volleying the ball to each other instead of throwing. Goals are score by volleying the ball at the goal. Both the header game and the volley game may be played with goalkeepers. Just widen to the width of regulation size goals

AREA: Between the 18 yd. box and the half-line. The width of the 18 yd. box.

5v5 (3 team) transition game

HOW TO PLAY: Three teams of five play a transition game in one half a field the width of the 18 yard box. The field is split into two halves. One team attacks another team's goal. If a shot is taken and the keeper saves it, the ball goes wide or over the goal, or a goal is scored, the team that was defending gets a ball quickly – from the goalkeeper and attacks the third team that was waiting on the other half of the field. Score the most goals within the designated playing period.

OBJECTIVE: *To improve quick transitions, possessing the ball in tight spaces, combination play, penetrating passes and finishing.

MATERIALS: cones, pinnies, poles or portable goals, balls.

AREA: One half the field the width of the 18 yard box.

5v5+4 wide neutrals

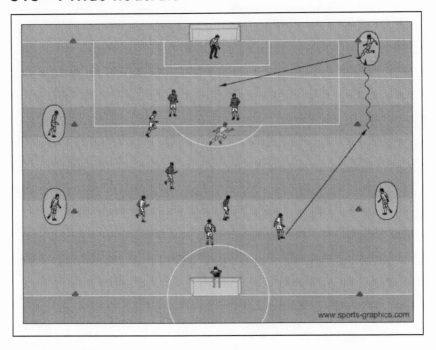

HOW TO PLAY: Two teams of five play a game in one half a field a bit wider than the width of the 18 yard box. Four neutral players are stationed on the outside of the playing area. The ball must be played to a neutral player before going to goal. Neutrals do not defend. Restarts are from the goalkeepers. Score the most goals within the designated playing period

OBJECTIVE: *To improve using the width, crossing and finishing.

MATERIALS: cones, pinnies, poles or portable goals, balls.

PROGRESSION: goals may only be scored from headers or volleys.

AREA: One half the field with 10 yard lanes in both wide areas.

4 goal game with random change of goals

HOW TO PLAY: In this game there are two teams of 8 players. Each team attacks a set of two goals. On the coaches' signal, the teams switch direction and attack the other two goals. The first team to score three goals wins.

OBJECTIVE: *To improve passing, support play, movement off the ball, perception, decision making and transition.

MATERIALS: cones, pinnies, balls

AREA: The entire area within the 18 yard box.

End line dribbling game (2v2, 3v3, or 4v4)

HOW TO PLAY: In this game there are two teams that must dribble the ball under control over the opponent's end line in order to score a point. The first team to reach three points is the winner.

OBJECTIVE: *To improve <u>dribbling</u>, <u>movement off the ball</u>, <u>combination play</u>, <u>perception</u> and <u>decision making</u>.

MATERIALS: cones, pinnies, balls

AREA: 3v3 – 20x30, 4v4 – 30x40, 5v5 – 40x50. The areas should be adjusted depending on the number of players and level of ability.

Dr. Tom Fleck's Barrel Ball

www.sports-graphics.com

HOW TO PLAY: In this game there are two teams that keep possession of the ball and try to attack any of the four garbage can goals. A ball that hits the garbage can on the ground =1 point while a ball that goes into the top of the garbage can =3 points. Rings of cones are placed around each garbage can, and no player may cross into the ring before the ball crosses in. If an attacking player goes in too early, there is a change of possession. If a defender goes in too early there is a penalty shot 12 paces away from the garbage can with no other players impeding.

OBJECTIVE: *To improve possession, switching the point of attack, and transition.

MATERIALS: cones, pinnies, balls

AREA: The cans are stationed in a square with no outside boundaries. The width between garbage cans depends on the number of players involved.

261

3v2 wave game with a big goal and two counter goals.

HOW TO PLAY: (3v2) The team of 18 is split into two groups with both keepers rotating in goal. The coach starts a new series by serving a ball to the three attackers who attack vs 2 defenders. The game is timed with the each team getting 5 minutes to attack the big goal. If possession is lost (ie. keeper makes a save or the ball is given away), the team defending the big goal transitions to attack and attempts to score on the two counter goals. This team may use their goalkeeper as another option, but he only has two touches. A new series (wave) begins if a goal is scored or if the ball crosses the touchline on either side. The team that ends up with the most goals within the allotted time wins. This game may also be played 2v1 with a narrower width.

OBJECTIVE: * Within the wave game players get many touches of the ball, they make decisions regarding where to run, at what angle to support the ball, when to penetrate and when to shoot on goal. Both teams learn to transition quickly when possession is gained or lost.

MATERIALS: cones, pinnies, balls   AREA: Half a field long and the width of the 18 yd box.

262

6 goal game (switching the point of attack)

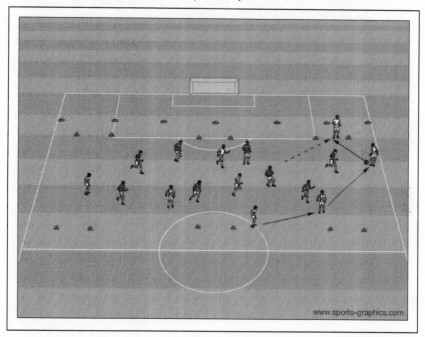

www.sports-graphics.com

HOW TO PLAY: In this game there are two teams of 7-8 players. Each team defends three goals and attacks three goals. The first team to score three goals wins the round.

OBJECTIVE: * Recognition where pressure is and switching the point of attack. Running from behind into forward positions. Passing, possession and penetration.

MATERIALS: cones, pinnies, balls

AREA: The area between the half line and the 18 yard box plus an extension of 6 yards for one of the two scoring zones. There are two six yard scoring zones behind the goals.

MORE SMALL-SIDED GAMES/GLOBAL GAMES

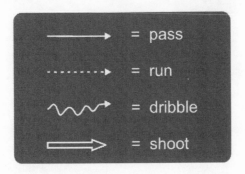

= pass

= run

= dribble

= shoot

FAKES/1V1 DRIBBLING
(even numbers)

Number of players: 10-18 (5-9 partners playing 1v1)

Area: 25x15 yards with two scoring zones 5x10 yards

Time: 6 - one minute rounds

How to play: 1v1 game in partners. To score a point the player with the ball must dribble by his opponent (using fakes) into the scoring zone. Each player attacks and defends a goal. After each goal there is a change of possession.

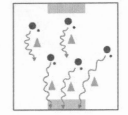

Number of players: 10-18 (5-9 partners playing 1v1)

Area: 20x20 yards with one 7 yard goal.

Time: 6 - one minute rounds

How to play: 1v1 game in partners. To score a point the player with the ball must dribble by his opponent (using fakes) and then through the gate (goal). After each goal there is a change of possession.

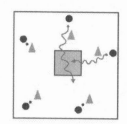

Number of players: 10-18 (5-9 partners playing 1v1)

Area: 20x20 yards with a 5 yard box as a scoring zone.

Time: 6 - one minute rounds

How to play: 1v1 game in partners. To score a point the player with the ball must dribble by his opponent into the scoring zone. Each player attacks and defends a goal. After each goal there is a change of possession.

FAKES/1v1 DRIBBLING

(numbers down)

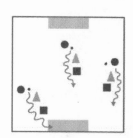

Number of players: 9 (3 partners playing 1v1 + 3 neutral defenders)

Area: 25x20 yards with two 5x10 scoring zones.

Time: 6 - one minute rounds

How to play: 1v1 game in partners + 1 neutral defender who always plays with the defender. After each minute the neutral changes roles. To score a point the player with the ball must dribble by his opponents into the scoring zone. After each goal there is a change of possession.

.

Number of players: 9 (3 partners playing 1v1 + 3 neutral defenders)

Area: 25x20 yards with four - 3 yard goals placed laterally within the area.

Time: 6 - one minute rounds

How to play: 1v1 game in partners + 1 neutral defender who always plays with the defender. After each minute the neutral changes roles. To score a point the player with the ball must dribble by his opponents through (either side of) any of the four - 3 yard goals. After each goal there is a change of possession.

FAKES/1V1 DRIBBLING

(numbers down)

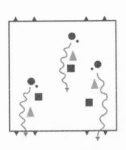

Number of players: 9 (3 partners playing 1v1 + 3 neutral defenders)

Area: 25x20 yards with 4 - three yard goals.

Time: 6 - one minute rounds

How to play: 1v1 game in partners + 1 neutral defender who always plays with the defender. After each minute the neutral changes roles. To score a point the player with the ball must dribble by his opponents through any of the four goals that he is attacking. After each goal there is a change of possession.

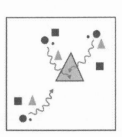

Number of players: 9 (3 partners playing 1v1 + 3 neutral defenders)

Area: 20x20 yards with 3 - three yard goals.

Time: 6 - one minute rounds

How to play: 1v1 game in partners + 1 neutral defender who always plays with the defender. After each minute the neutral changes roles. To score a point the player with the ball must dribble by his opponents through (either side of) any of the three goals. After each goal there is a change of possession.

Number of players: 9 (3 partners playing 1v1 + 3 neutral defenders)

Area: 25x25 yards with 1 (7 yard) triangular goal in the middle of the area.

Time: 6 - one minute rounds

How to play: 1v1 game in partners + 1 neutral defender who always plays with the defender. After each minute the neutral changes roles. To score a point the player with the ball must dribble by his opponents through the triangular goal. After each goal there is a change of possession.

266

PASSING

(numbers up)

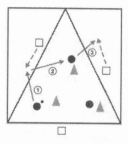

<u>Number of players</u>: 9 (3v3 + 3 neutrals)

<u>Area</u>: A 15x15x15 - triangle.

<u>Time</u>: 3 - three minute rounds

<u>How to play</u>: 3v3+3 neutrals who support the team in possession on the outside of the triangle. Neutrals may move around the perimeter of the triangle to support the ball. After 3 minutes the neutrals change roles. The game is <u>one</u> touch.

<u>Number of players</u>: 10 (4v4 + 2 neutrals)

<u>Area</u>: 50x50 yard area divided into four quadrants of 25x25.

<u>Time</u>: 10 minutes

<u>How to play</u>: 4v4+2 neutrals who support the team in possession of the ball. The team in possession must make four passes on the inside of a quadrant before passing to another quadrant. Each time a team is successful playing four passes and then keeps the ball by passing to another quadrant they earn a point. The game is <u>one</u> touch.

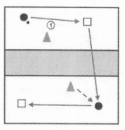

<u>Number of players</u>: 6 (2v2 + 2 neutrals)

<u>Area</u>: 30x15 yard area with 3 divided into three 10x15 zones.

<u>Time</u>: 3 rounds of three minutes

<u>How to play</u>: 2v2+2 neutrals who support the team in possession of the ball. Every three minutes change the neutrals. The field is divided into three zones. (Two wide zones and a central zone where the ball cannot be played. A team may only make four passes in one zone before having to pass to the opposite zone.

267

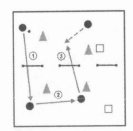

Number of players: 10 (4v4+ 2 neutrals)

Area: 30x30 yard area with three 2 yard goals.

Time: 5 rounds of two minutes

How to play: 4v4+2 neutrals who support the team in possession of the ball on each side of the area. Every three minutes change the neutrals. The team in possession earns a point each time one of its players completes a pass through one of the three goals. They then continue in possession.

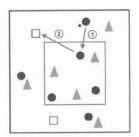

Number of players: 14 (6v6 + 2 neutrals)

Area: 40x40 yard area with a central zone of 20x20 yards.

Time: 2 rounds of five minutes

How to play: 6v6+2 neutrals who support the team in possession of the ball. Each team puts three players within the 20x20 zone and three players outside of this zone. The team in possession earns a point each time they complete ten consecutive passes. They then continue in possession. After five minutes change the position of the players.

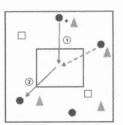

Number of players: 10 (4v4+ 2 neutrals)

Area: 35x35 yard area with one 7x7 box in the middle.

Time: 10 minutes

How to play: 4v4+2 neutrals who support the team in possession of the ball. The team in possession earns a point each time one of its players completes a pass from the inside of the central zone. They then continue in possession.

268

PASSING
(even numbers)

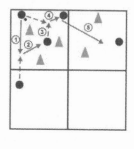

Number of players: 10 (5v5)

Area: 40x40 yard area divided into four quadrants of 20x20.

Time: 10 minutes

How to play: 5v5. The team in possession must make four passes in one quadrant before passing into another quadrant. Each time they are successful doing so they earn a point.

Number of players: 10 (5v5)

Area: 60x40 yard area divided into three zones of 20x40.

Time: 10 minutes

How to play: 5v5. The field is divided in three zones of 20x40. The team in possession must make four passes in one zone before passing into another zone. Each time they are successful doing so they earn a point.

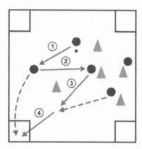

Number of players: 10 (5v5)

Area: 40x30 yard area with four 7x7 boxes.

Time: 10 minutes

How to play: 5v5. The field is divided in three zones of 20x40. The team in possession earns a point each time they are able to pass the ball to a teammate within one of the four boxes. They then maintain possession of the ball.

269

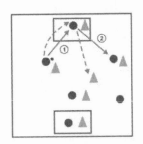

Number of players: 12 (6v6)

Area: 40x35 yard area with two 10x5 boxes.

Time: 10 minutes

How to play: 6v6. Each team places one player in each of the two boxes. The team in possession earns a point by completing ten consecutive passes. They then maintain possession. Each time a pass is made to a player inside one of the 5x5 boxes, another player moves to take his place.

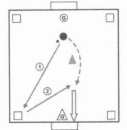

SHOOTING
(numbers up)

Number of players: 10 (2 teams of 2 players with four neutrals + 2 goalkeepers)

Area: 20x15 yard area with two – regular goals with goalkeepers.

Time: 12 rounds of 1 minute each

How to play: 2v2 + 4 neutrals that play with the team in possession. There are two regular goals with goalkeepers. The team in possession must shoot before making four passes. Change the neutrals frequently. The coach should supply balls in order to maintain the proper flow. Restart from the goalkeeper.

Number of players: 7 (2v2 + 2 neutrals + 1 goalkeeper)

Area: Penalty area with one regular goal.

Time: 6 rounds of two minutes each

How to play: 2v2 +2 neutrals that support the team in possession on the lateral areas of the penalty area. Change the neutrals often. Each team attacks and defends the goal. The team in possession must shoot before making four passes. The coach should supply balls in order to maintain the proper flow. Restart from the coach.

SHOOTING
(numbers up)

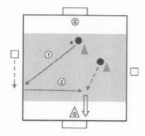

Number of players: 8 (2 teams of 3 players + 2 neutrals)

Area: 40x20 with a 20x20 middle zone.

Time: 6 rounds of two minutes each

How to play: 3v3 +2 neutrals that support the team in possession from each of the touchlines. Every two minutes change the neutrals. Each team attacks and defends a regular goal. The team in possession must shoot before making four passes and the player shooting must be within the 20x20 middle zone. The coach should supply balls in order to maintain the proper flow. Restart from the goalkeeper.

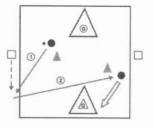

Number of players: 8 (2 teams of 3 players + 2 neutrals)

Area: 25x20 with two (7x7x7) triangular goals with a goalkeeper in each triangular goal.

Time: 6 rounds of two minutes each

How to play: 3v3 +2 neutrals that play with the team in possession from each of the touchlines. Every two minutes change the neutrals. Each team attacks and defends a triangular goal. The team in possession must shoot before making four passes. The coach should supply balls in order to maintain the proper flow. Restart from the goalkeeper. If a save is made the ball is distributed to the team defending the shot.

Number of players: 11 (2 teams of 4 players + 3 neutrals)

Area: 40x20 with a central zone of 20x20 and two regular goals.

Time: 6 rounds of two minutes each

How to play: 4v4 +3 neutrals that play with the team in possession from inside the field. Change the neutrals frequently. Each team attacks and defends a regular goal. The team in possession must shoot before making four passes. The coach should supply balls in order to maintain the proper flow. Restart from the goalkeeper.

SHOOTING
(even numbers)

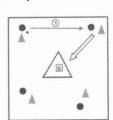

Number of players: 10 (2 teams of 5 players)

Area: 40x20 with a central zone of 20x20 and two regular goals.

Time: 3 rounds of three minutes each

How to play: 5v5 including goalkeepers. Each team attacks and defends a regular goal. The team in possession must shoot before making four passes. The coach should supply balls in order to maintain the proper flow. Restart from the goalkeeper.

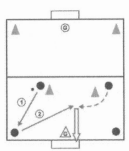

Number of players: 9 (2 teams of 4 players + 1 goalkeeper)

Area: 35x35 with a (7x7x7) triangular goal.

Time: 3 rounds of three minutes each

How to play: 4v4 Each team attacks and defends the triangular goal. The team in possession must shoot before making four passes. The coach should supply balls in order to maintain the proper flow. Restart from the goalkeeper. If a save is made the ball is distributed to the team defending the shot.

Number of players: 10 (2 teams of 5 players)

Area: 30x20 with two regular goals.

Time: 4 rounds of two minutes each

How to play: (5v5) Each team attacks and defends a regular goal. Each team places two players in the corners to support the play as target players. Every two minutes change the players in the corners. The team in possession must shoot before making four passes. The coach should supply balls in order to maintain the proper flow. Restart from the goalkeeper. If a save is made the ball is distributed to the team defending the shot.

La Bombonera: Home of Boca Juniors – Buenos Aires, Argentina.[27]

27 Photograph: Steve Newton – Wikimedia Commons 2009.

✪ A futsal goal.[28]

---

[28] Photograph: Chong Fat (GNU Free Documentation License) Wikimedia Commons - 2009.

CHAPTER 24

Futsal

"If fútbol is the King of Sports, futsal is the Queen of Sports."
– Cony Konstin (FIFA Futsal Instructor)

HISTORY[29]

Futsal is a smaller version of soccer played on a court with dimensions: 25-42 yards long by 15-25 yards wide. Futsal's beginnings can be found in Montevideo, Uruguay, in South America. It was in the 1930's when the Uruguayan, Juan Carlos Ceriani, invented a 5v5 version of soccer for youth competitions at YMCAs in Montevideo. He had seen youth playing soccer on basketball courts, and decided to adapt the basketball court by adding goals in order to replicate a smaller version of the game of soccer. Uruguay had recently become

---

[29] United States Futsal Federation (www.futsal.com)

world champions in 1930, and the game at the time was extremely popular. One of the principle reasons behind Ceriani's modified soccer game was to help the national team of Uruguay better prepare for future World Cups. He believed that players playing futsal would be able to develop agility, and physical quickness along with the ability to think quicker since they would be playing the game in tighter spaces. The term "futsal" is the global term used for the game, and it is a combination of the Spanish word, fútbol and the Spanish root word for "indoor" or "room", salón or sala. Futsal is also referred to as Fútbol Sala in Spain.

"Futsal will always be my first love." – Ronaldo
(Three time World Player of The Year and World Champion – Brazil)

After getting it's start during the 1930's in Uruguay, futsal quickly gained popularity throughout South America, especially in the country of Brazil. Some of Brazil's greatest players in fact grew up playing futsal. Pelé, Zico, Socrates, Rivelino, and Ronaldinho all developed their skills in the 5v5 game. While Brazil is still the center of the futsal universe, the game is now overseen by FIFA and played in all parts of the world.

The first Futsal World Championship was run by FIFUSA (Federação International de Futebol de Salão) and was held in Sao Paulo, Brazil, in 1982, with Brazil winning the championship. The Brazilians also won at the World Championship in held in 1985 in Madrid, Spain, but ended up losing in the third World Championship held in 1988 in Australia to Paraguay. FIFA took over the responsibility for running the futsal World Championship in 1989 in Holland and 1992 in Hong Kong. Brazil won both of these respective championships. The United States Futsal team, finished third in 1989 and runners up in 1992. The Third FIFA World Futsal Championship was held in 1996 in Spain.

United States Futsal has continued to hold a yearly National Championship for over 27 years beginning in the year 1985. Futsal is becoming more established at the youth level in the U.S., and the Boys and Girls Clubs of America have been leaders in promoting the sport in the United States. The Columbia Park Club in San Francisco, for example, was the first to be asked by the U.S. Futsal Federation to present a futsal demonstration. Subsequently, the national organization adopted the sport, and it is now played at 1,100 Boys and Girls Clubs throughout the U.S.

BENEFITS

The benefits of futsal with regards to player development are astronomic. The more that we can get our youngsters playing futsal, the more creative, and confident they will be with the ball at their feet. They will also significantly improve speed of thought and decision making; areas that will make the transition to the outdoor 11v11 game that much easier. On the following pages I have included a basic introduction to futsal with information on the benefits for player development, basic rules, and the dimensions of the court.

☆ South America – The birthplace of futsal.[30]

---

[30] Artwork: Copyright Expired - Wikimedia Commons.

THE BENEFITS OF FUTSAL

☆ twelve times more touches of the ball than in soccer makes the game more fun for children as well as adults.

☆ the creation of countless 1v1 duels.

☆ the development of game intelligence through constant changes in tactical situations.

☆ emphasis on skill rather than on physical contact.

☆ improves speed of thought, speed of movement and speed of play.

☆ improves agility

☆ less expensive option due to low maintenance costs.

DIFFERENCES BETWEEN SOCCER AND FUTSAL

FUTSAL (FIFA INDOOR SOCCER)	SOCCER
5 players	11 players
Size 4 ball with 30% reduced bounce	Size 5 ball
Unlimited "flying substitutions"	3 substitutions
Kick in	Throw in
Stopped clock	Running clock
No body contact	Body contact allowed
No offside	Offside rule applied
One play back to keeper's feet	Unlimited back passes to 'keeper (as long as keeper does not handle the back passed ball)
5 "accumulated foul" limit	Unlimited fouls
Sent off player can be substituted after 2 minutes or after opponent has scored	No substitution allowed for players sent off
20 minute halves (subjective to leagues)	45 minute halves

"No time plus no space equals better skills. Futsal is our national laboratory of improvisation." – Dr. Emilio Miranda (Professor of soccer at the University of São Paolo – Brazil.)

🜨 A futsal match between Brazil and Argentina.[31]

[31] Photograph: Released to public domain by Sportingn - Wikimedia Commons 2008.

DIMENSIONS OF A FUTSAL COURT

If official dimensions are required , you are advise to use metric measurements.

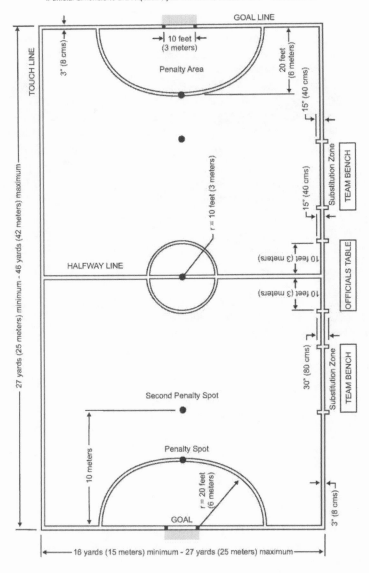

FUT · SAL/ESPAÑA'85

II CAMPEONATO MUNDIAL DE FUTBOL SALA

"FUTSY" EL ZORRO
MASCOTA OFICIAL DEL MUNDIAL

CHAPTER 25

Lighting the Fire: Encouraging Play Away From the Structured Practice

"Nothing great was ever achieved without enthusiasm."
— Ralph Waldo Emerson (American writer)

According to the Swedish psychologist Anders Ericsson, it takes approximately 10,000 hours in order to master a specific skill such as playing an instrument, a Martial Art, Chess or any other skill. The same is true for the sport of soccer. To put this in perspective it would take practicing three hours a day every day (365 days a year) for ten years to become a master soccer player. Perhaps the main reason why our players have trouble competing at the highest levels internationally is the lack of time they spend outside of practice time playing with friends or on their own. In comparison to the top soccer nations, many of our players simply do not put in the amount of time necessary to compete at the top levels. One reason for the lack of soccer hours is due to the predominance of multisport athletes. While at the Brazilian CBF training center, I asked one of the coaches up to

what age the CBF recommended children participate in various sports before beginning to specialize. He answered in bewilderment "What do you mean, there is only <u>one</u> sport." He did actually change his response a moment later when he said "Well, there are various sports we recommend – futsal, beach soccer, soccer tennis, street soccer etc..."
It is true that the Brazilian soccer culture is something that runs so deep that it is found in almost every fabric of Brazilian society. I remember being amazed that the beaches in Botafogo – Rio de Janeiro had lights, goals and games going on at all hours of the day and night. Futsal courts were accessible everywhere in urban park areas where children entertained themselves for hours playing pick-up games. I have also seen this kind of passion for the sport in places like Cornelius, Oregon where the parks are always packed with players playing soccer young and old with balls rolling in the streets.

It is clear that the amount of soccer culture within our country varies from one community to the next. There is no doubt that the home culture can have a lot to do with how much a child plays away from the structured training sessions. Children, for example, who come from "soccer first" families tend to play more with their parents, relatives and friends at home than children who come from families where soccer is not the most important sport. Since many of our latino children come from "soccer first" families, they end up playing more hours at home and they tend to develop higher technical skill and a better sense of the game. Something is transmitted from the family members to the younger generation of children. According to author Daniel Coyle within certain environments in countries such as Brazil, a fire is lit in the children by the culture itself, leading in many cases to the development of a deeper passion and commitment to practicing the sport. This is the same type of fire that we see taking place with many of our soccer first families in the United States.

Times are certainly changing within the soccer community in the United States. Every day there are more and more parents who may not have come from a soccer first family, but who have nevertheless grown up understanding and loving the game and who are passing it on to their children. With this said, it seems to me that if we really want to help our players develop a higher level of play, nothing is as important as finding ways to light the fire of passion and commitment to the sport. Encouraging play away from the structured training sessions is one way to help light this fire. <u>On the following pages is a list of ideas.</u>

✪ Various players from Subbuteo Table Soccer.[32]

---

[32]Photograph: Released to public domain by Sportingn - Wikimedia Commons 2008.

1. ALLOW TIME FOR FREE PLAY AND JUGGLING AT THE REGULAR TRAINING SESSION IN ORDER TO MODEL WHAT WE WANT OUR PLAYERS TO DO OUTSIDE OF TRAINING.

The more players are exposed to free play or they are given free time with a ball to juggle, the more they will want to do the same activities outside of the structured training session.

2. ENCOURAGE PLAYERS TO FIND A SCHOOL OR PARK NEAR THEIR HOME THAT IS A SAFE PLACE TO PLAY.

Ideally this place will have a cement area to play small-sided games, and a wall for practicing passing, receiving, juggling and shooting. A tennis court can be used to play soccer tennis. *see chapter on alternate training area.

★ A school courtyard with ready made goals under the water fountains.

3. PUT PLAYERS ON YOUR TEAM INTO A SMALL GROUP FREE PLAY BUDDY SYSTEM BASED ON LOCATION.

In this way players will be able to get together with fellow teammates at a location closer to their own house on days when there is no team training. Groups of 4 players will allow for simplified games of 1v1 and 2v2. Invite friends from the player's local school(s) to come out when they can in order to build the number of players.

4. HAVE PARENT VOLUNTEERS OR AN ASSISTANT COACH ROTATE SUPERVISING FREE PLAY DAYS.

The team first needs to find a location such as a park or a school. During the free play days there is no coaching. The players bring their own balls and are provided with some cones to make their own goals. Parent volunteers would need to register with the club as a volunteer coach. They would supervise in pairs once every two months depending on how many free days are required. Teams split into groups of (3, 4, 5) players and play rotating games. Those who are not in the game can do wall work or juggling. This free play day can also be set up between teams of the same age group with a buddy clubs.

5. HAVE THE TEAM PERIODICALLY RENT A FUTSAL COURT AND PLAY FUTSAL INSTEAD OF HAVING A REGULAR TRAINING SESSION.

If playing outside is not an option and all local indoor basketball courts are taken then the next best thing would be to pool resources and rent a futsal court. If there are no futsal specific courts just rent an indoor court and play futsal rules.

6. HAVE YOUR PLAYERS WATCH YOUTUBE VIDEOS TO GET THEM EXCITED ABOUT PRACTICING NEW MOVES, OR TO ENCOURAGE THEM TO IMAGINE THEY ARE THEIR FAVORITE STAR PLAYER.

7. ENCOURAGE YOUR PLAYERS TO MAKE A HOMEMADE BALL TO USE AROUND THE HOUSE

(Here are the instructions on how to make a homemade ball.)

1. The first page of the newspaper is crumpled up and squeezed tightly. This becomes the core.

2. Next, wrap three more sheets around the existing core.

3. Wrap athletic tape around the core in the form of a cross.

4. Add three more sheets of newspaper.

5. Then wrap the athletic tape around it until the newspaper is covered up.

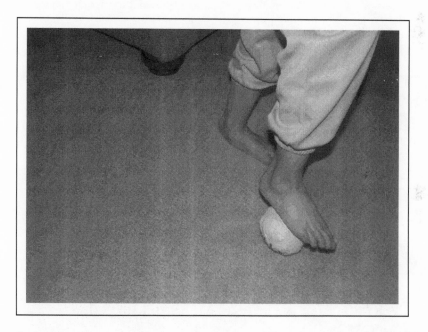

"Everything I have achieved in football is due to playing in the streets with my friends." - Zinedane Zidane (Former legendary player with Real Madrid and France)

8. REQUEST THAT PLAYERS GO TO THE iSOCCER WEBSITE TO HELP MOTIVATE THEM TO MONITOR THEIR OWN PROGRESS IN VARIOUS TECHNICAL AREAS.

www.isoccer.org

Players are motivated when they can see tangible improvements in their game. The iSoccer methodology includes specific assessments that allow players to compete against themselves in order to beat their previous top score. Players can also set goals for future improvement. The more they practice, the more they will improve their overall technical ability.

9. INVITE PLAYERS GO TO THE WEBSITE WWW.TECHNICAFOOTBALL.COM TO GET NEW IDEAS FOR PLAYING SOCCER AT HOME.

This website from Denmark (in English) is full of short video clips of ideas for playing soccer at home. The author, Jannik Riis, is embassador for Danish Football, a teacher, and a UEFA A licensed coach.

10. EVERY SO OFTEN HAVE THE PLAYERS RUN THEIR OWN PRACTICE SESSION

11. CHALLENGE TEAMS FROM OTHER CLUBS TO 3V3, 5v5 or 7v7 FRIENDLIES RATHER THAN PLAYING 11V11.

✫ "Potrero" - Street soccer in Buenos Aires, Argentina.[33]

[33] Photo: David Weekly - Wikimedia Commons 2007.

CHAPTER 26

Great Players to Emulate

Emulation is defined as the ambition to equal or excel. Here is a list of great attacking players that our young players should learn about and emulate. There are without a doubt many others that could be added to the list. In countries with a soccer history such as Argentina, Brazil, Spain, Holland, Germany and Italy, the young players have plenty of idols to emulate and copy. This may not always be the case for young players in this country. Today our players have access to much more soccer on television than in the past, and they are learning much more about famous teams and players. Many have a favorite player or team that they follow on a regular basis. As a coach and mentor, it would be worthwhile giving one's players a fun assignment every so often to seek out information on one of these players, watch them on You tube and write a report on the player. See list on the following page.

Pelé	Sergio Kun Aguero	Elias Figueroa
Maradona	Robinho	Paolo Futre
Johan Cruyff	Diego Forlan	Bernd Schuster
Marco Van Basten	Neymar	Hristo Stoichkov
Garrincha	Leonel Messi	Jurgen Klinsmann
Zico	Andres Iniesta	Ronaldo
Alfredo di Stéfano	Xavi Hernandez	Samuel Eto
Rivelino	Pablo Aimar	Kanu
Tostao	Ferenc Puskas	Rui Costa
Teofilo Cubillas	Franz Beckenbauer	Claudio Pizarro
Eusebio	Omar Sivori	Cesar Cueto
Gabriel Batistuta	Ronaldinho	Mágico Gonzalez
Enzo Francescoli	Norberto Alonso	Carlos Alberto
Ivan Zamorano	Zito	Jairzinho
Socrates	Ruben Sosa	Rivaldo
Roberto Falcao	Cristiano Ronaldo	Zlatan Ibrahimovic
George Weah	David Villa	Hugo Sotil
Bruno Conti	Roberto Carlos	Klaus Fischer
Abedi Pelé Ayew	Didier Drogba	Ramon Diaz
Romario	Ryan Giggs	Eder
Michel Platini	Cesc Fabregas	Marcelo Salas
Dennis Bergkamp	Eden Hazard	Alexis Sanchez
Eric Cantona	Deco	Nani
George Best	Fernando Torres	Adebayour
Luis Figo	Mario Kempes	Bobby Charlton
Michael Laudrup	Andres Pirlo	Carlos Valderrama
Hugo Sanchez	Landon Donovan	Osvaldo Ardiles
Zinedine Zidane	Hidetoshi Nakata	Thierry Henry
Ruud Gullit	Emilio Butragueño	Georgi Kinkladze
Gheorge Hagi	Jay Jay Okocha	Robert Pires

Imagining an All-time 11 Team

In order to help create a deeper soccer culture amongst our players, I recommend giving them a fun assignment to investigate and form an all-time 11 team. In doing the investigation and completing this kind of activity, the players will learn about some of the great players in the game and will write briefly about why they chose each player. This activity also promotes dialogue amongst our players as they talk about who is on each other's their team. Ultimately the goal is to encourage our players to learn about and emulate the greats of the game. Some will say that it is unrealistic to name one team of 11 players because there are so many differences in the way the game was played in different eras. I tend agree with this, but on another level I still think it is a lot of fun putting together an all-time 11 and great for our players to learn about the top players of different eras. Just for fun I have put an all-time 11 on the following page.

* Although there are many world-class women's players for our players to watch, former Women's World Cup Champion coach Anson Dorrance believes that female soccer players must watch the men's game and use it as a learning laboratory. He believes that women soccer players don't spend nearly enough time watching the men's games on television.

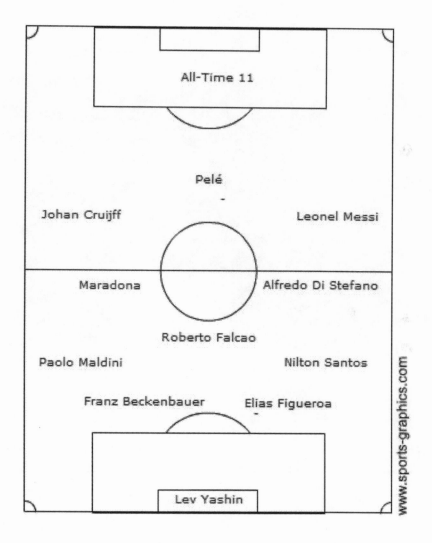

All-Time 11

Pelé

Johan Cruijff   Leonel Messi

Maradona   Alfredo Di Stefano

Roberto Falcao

Paolo Maldini   Nilton Santos

Franz Beckenbauer   Elias Figueroa

Lev Yashin

www.sports-graphics.com

ZICO

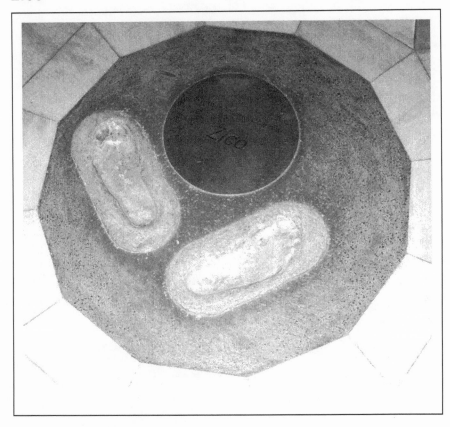

☆ Zico's footprints inside Maracanã Stadium in Rio de Janeiro, Brazil.
One of the all-time great attacking players. (1982 World Player of the Year.)

CHAPTER 27

Juggling – Romance With the Ball

"I don't believe that skill was, or ever will be, the result of coaches. It is a result of a love affair between the child and the ball." – Manfred Schellscheidt (Former United States National Team Coach at various levels)

As we look for areas to improve the level of the game in the United States, we must aim high and continually ask ourselves how to encourage the development of more technical players. It is well known that in Latin America there is a premium placed on technical skill. Year after year top Latin American players are seen playing for top European Clubs who are willing to pay for such talent. Argentina and Brazil export more top flight players than any other countries in the world. During my time observing professional youth academies in South America, it became clear to me that juggling is used frequently as a means of developing and fine tuning the control of the ball. It was obvious that the players I observed had spent many hundreds of hours outside of structured training on their own with the ball. Including juggling during a training session not only helps to improve and fine tune technique, but it also helps encourage the player's romance with the ball that plays to the spirit of the inner child.

When visiting the (CBF) Brazilian National Training Center outside of Rio de Janeiro, I observed a pre-warm up in which 14 year old players started juggling a ping-pong size ball, and then progressed to a tennis ball, a Brazilian rubber ball, and finally a regulation size ball. On another visit to South America while observing at the Tahuichi Academy in Bolivia, I observed various youth players from U6 to U17 practicing various levels of juggling. The younger players began with the age/skill appropriate technique of toss - juggle - catch, while the older players walked while juggling tennis balls. In Argentina during an observation of Club Atlético Independiente's first team training I observed players juggling at the beginning of practice alternating between a tennis ball and regulation sized ball. It is clear that juggling is used at all levels of soccer from youth players all the way up to first team professionals. Incorporating a juggling routine in a practice has the secondary effect of bringing down the players anxiety and raising their motivation level. Any youngster who loves soccer will tell you that they enjoy spending time with a ball.

It is important to follow a progression where players are expected to do what their present skill level will allow. When working with beginners, the goal should be to juggle once and catch. The progression could be toss-right foot laces-catch, toss-left foot laces-catch, toss-right thigh-catch, toss-left thigh-catch, toss-head-catch and repeat. If having young children practicing with the head, then the ball should be slightly deflated or even replaced by a softer plastic ball. When working with beginners, the coach should make sure to teach the players to keep the mouth closed and eyes open. The activity may begin stationary and then continue while players are moving. As players progress the coach may ask them to attempt to add an extra juggle before they catch the ball. Our players should be encouraged to spend time each day trying to keep the ball up. Some may be motivated by attempting to keep the ball up a record number of times. Programs, such as I-Soccer, are a good way to have players measure their own individual progress. When a player is motivated to continually better his previous score, progress can be made quite rapidly in a short amount of time.

Once players are more comfortable with keeping the ball in the air, they should next begin working with a juggling routine with patterns. It is important to note that keeping the ball in the air for a set number of times is a step in the progression of controlling the ball, but the more advanced step demands that the player be able to put the ball exactly where he or she wants it to go. This is much more challenging. A coach may also send out links to www.youtube.com videos on how to perform freestyle tricks that a player may add to his or her routine.

★ A statue of the "El Principe" Enzo Francescoli
inside River Plate's Estadio Monumental
in Buenos Aires, Argentina.

PATTERN JUGGLING

(INTERMEDIATE TO ADVANCED PLAYERS)

50 times with Right foot Laces

50 times with Left foot Laces

1 high touch and 1 low touch

juggling below knee height

juggling below knee height + clapping the hands in rhythm <u>each</u> time you touch the ball

juggling from the foot to hip height

juggling from the foot to head height

pattern of 2 touches with right foot and 1 touch with left foot

pattern of 2 touches with left foot and 1 touch with right foot

pattern of 1 touch with right foot laces and 1 touch with left thigh

pattern of 1 touch with Left Foot Laces and 1 touch with right. thigh

3 touches and 1 high touch and control/deaden with laces

360 spin + sit down/stand up juggling challenges

360 spin

While juggling put the ball high in the air and do a 360 spin and continue juggling. Another even more difficult challenge is to juggle, put the ball high in the air, sit down, stand up and continue juggling without the ball hitting the ground. The player must bend his knees and crouch down to get in a sitting position, then he must juggle until he is ready to stand up, put the ball high in the air and stand up quickly in order to not let the ball drop.

Around the World

Juggle beginning with one touch right foot laces, one touch inside right foot, one touch laces, one touch outside right foot, one touch right thigh, one touch right shoulder, one touch head, one touch left shoulder, one touch left thigh, one touch left foot laces, one touch inside left foot, one touch left foot laces, one touch outside left foot – repeat.

Numbers Juggling

Two players juggle one ball between them. Player A takes one juggle and then passes to player B. Player B takes one juggle and passes back to player A. Player A now takes two juggles before passing to player B, the sequence continues to ten and then restarts again with one. Variation: Each player can also call a random number for the partner to juggle.

Juggling Wars

Two players each juggle a ball. Each tries to knock his partner's ball to the ground with the foot while continuing to juggle his own ball. The winner is the player who keeps the ball in the air the longest. If one player succeeds in knocking his partner's ball to the ground, but has his own ball drop at the same time, the game starts again with both players lifting the ball and juggling.

Task juggling

Two players juggle one ball. After receiving the ball from his partner, the player who just received the ball calls out "forward roll", "backwards roll", "360 spin" "pushup" "jump and head" etc… and the player who just passed the ball must perform the action before receiving the ball again. How long can they keep the ball up?

"The most important aspect of our program is always ball work. In all exercises the players do, whether it's physical preparation or any other kind of training, the ball is always there." – Albert Benaiges (Former coordinator of the Barcelona Youth Academy)

Group Juggling stationary/moving

Split a team of 18 into three groups of 6 and have each group hold hands and juggle the ball in the group. (stationary) If the ball drops start again from zero. The team with the most consecutive juggles in a designated time period wins. Next have the same groups compete against each other by walk/jog while juggling the ball. The first to complete the designated course is the winner.

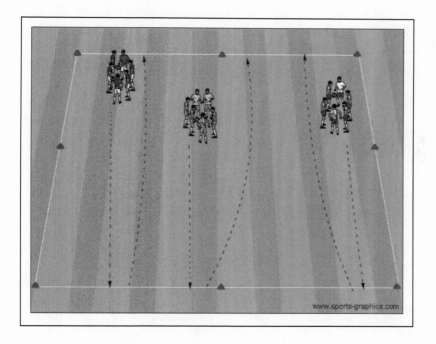

Line Juggling

Split a team of 18 into three groups of 6. Each group splits into two groups of three players who face each other two yards apart. One player lifts the ball to the opposite line and goes to the end of the opposite line. The ball is juggled back and forth between the lines. The teams keep track of the maximum number of juggles during a period of time. The winner is the team with the most consecutive juggles in a designated time period. This activity can be limited to the head only.

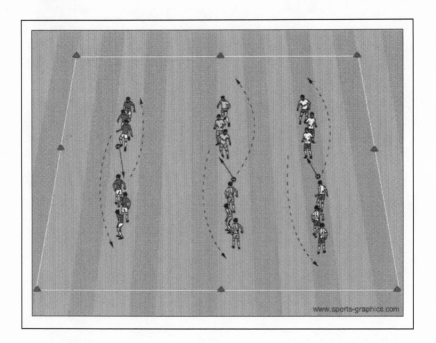

Walking with the ball

End line to the edge of the 18 – The player should lift the ball up and walk with it for a set distance. How far can you go without the ball dropping? If you are at a lined field, walk while juggling from the end line to the edge of the 18 yard box, turn and go back. If the ball drops go to the closest line and continue. Each length counts as a point. Go for 5 minutes. If a player achieves 15 lengths in 5 minutes, then it is time for a smaller ball.

www.sports-graphics.com

Juggling Course

Set up a number of gates or obstacles that players must juggle through or around. If the ball drops, the player must go back to the start (end of the line). Split team into two groups. The players juggle through the course and then shoot on goal. This may be done as a competition with each team juggling for five minutes on each side right and left. Count how many goals are scored. The ball must hit the back of the net.

CHAPTER 28

Wall Routine – Repetition and Imagination

"If tennis, baseball, volleyball, and basketball are sports in which players use repetition to improve specific skills, why not use a wall with measurements of a goal, where each player can practice finishing 50 times a week, 200 times per month, 2,000 times in ten months until he or she becomes an expert finisher."

– ATFA (Association of Argentine Football Coaches)

This is a fun and highly effective way of improving the technical areas of a player's game when away from the team training sessions. The primary reason for its effectiveness is that the wall allows for a large volume of repetition. As a player spends more time at a wall, the more comfortable the player will be with the ball when playing in games. This ultimately helps improve a player's control and speed of play.

A WALL ROUTINE

When practicing a routine, it is very important and thus targets should be used. One may use the existing natural lines in the wall as targets or draw lines on the wall with washable playground chalk.

✪ A training wall in Fremont, California – United States.

PASSING FOCUS (AIM FOR A TARGET)

These exercises should be made age appropriate. Very young players still developing should not be required to play one touch. Distance 10-12 yards from the wall. The distance may be adjusted so as to be appropriate for the player's age, size and strength. Reminders: *When passing with the inside of the foot, the ankle should be locked and the toes of the foot contacting the ball should be slightly pointed up. The plant foot should be towards the target. When passing with the laces the toes of the foot contacting the ball should be pointing down while the plant foot points towards the target.*

☒ 100 one touch passes inside right foot

☒ 100 one touch passes inside left foot

☒ 100 one touch laces right foot

☒ 100 one touch laces left foot

RECEIVING FOCUS

Distance 5-7 yards from the wall

☒ Hit the ball hard against the wall and receive with the inside of the foot cushioning the ball. After 100 repetitions one side then do 100 with the opposite foot. The receiving foot should hardly contact the ball. Imagine that the ball is made of glass and will break if not received softly enough.

☒ Volley the ball against the wall and receive with thigh, abdomen, chest, or head and then bring to the ground. 100 repetitions.

PASSING AND RECEIVING FOCUS (AIM FOR A TARGET)

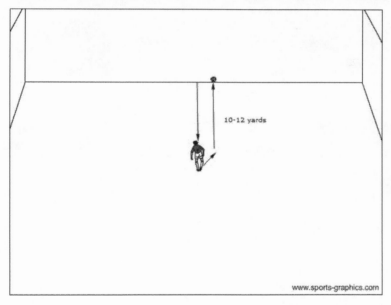

Distance 10-12 yards from the wall

PELÉ

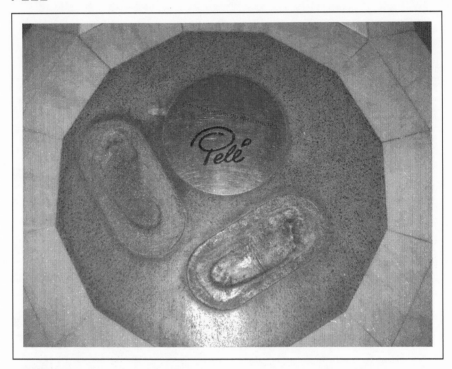

★ The great Pelé's footprints inside Maracanã Stadium – Rio de Janeiro, Brazil. Pelé is the only three time World Cup Champion and named FIFA player of the century.

☒ 100 two touch receive outside of right foot / step right foot / step left foot (plant foot) / pass inside of right foot

☒ 100 two touch receive outside of left foot / step left foot / step right foot (plant foot) / pass inside of left foot.

☒ Chip the ball 100 times to the wall and as it comes back bouncing, adjust your body position forward or backward, cover the ball so it stops bouncing and rolls to one side of your body, then pass to a target. Alternate right and left feet.

"I would also hit the ball against the side of the house...
Hitting the ball with both feet, seeing how long I could return the wall
passes without losing control. I found out later that so many pros
spend lots of their childhood doing that." – Dennis Bergkamp
(Former player Ajax, Arsenal and Holland)

SHOOTING FOCUS (AIM FOR A TARGET)

☒ Shoot at a target from varying distances. The target may be a drawing of a regulation size goal or simply various circles or boxes in different positions. (100 repetitions.) Practice bending the ball – inside and outside of both feet.

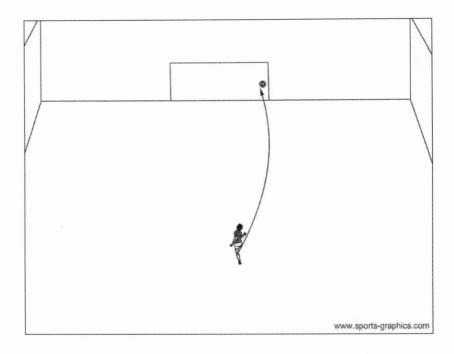

☒ Juggle the ball 3-4 times with your back to the wall, on the last juggle play it up in the air, in one motion cover the ball (settle it on the ground) with either inside or outside of the foot and turn and shoot at the target.

Alternate turning right and left and practice both feet.

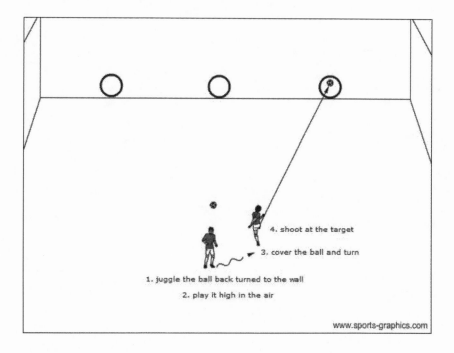

☒ Place an object such as a moveable bench (imagine this is the goalkeeper) about 10 yards from the wall. Dribble in at an angle and then lift the ball over the bench in order to score. Work inside and outside of both feet.

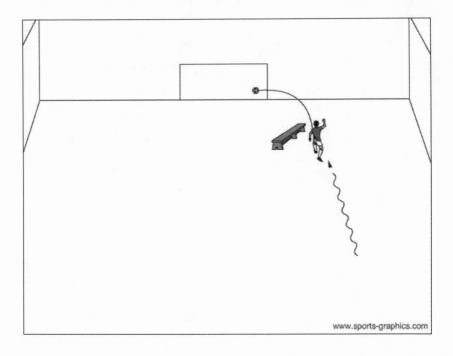

www.sports-graphics.com

VOLLEYING FOCUS

Distance volleying 10-12 yards away

The skill of volleying can be used for clearances, passing, or shooting at goal. If the goal is practicing clearances the trajectory of the ball should be up in the air. If the goal is passing or shooting the trajectory of the ball should be toward a target straight forward or down.

☒ Toss the ball up in the air and volley it first time against the wall. The toss may be made directly in front of the body or to either side. If the ball is tossed directly in front of the body the toe of the foot contacting the ball should be pointing slightly down. The plant foot should be pointing towards the target and contact made with the laces. If the ball is tossed from the side, the player must remember to dip the shoulder farthest from the ball in order to get over the ball and keep the trajectory down. Contact should be made with the laces. Both types of volleys from the front and from the side may be practiced on a half bounce.

☒ Juggle the ball as long as you can against the wall. Depending on skill level, this may be done with one or two bounces or for more advanced players with no bounces. Practice juggling against the wall with the inside of each foot and with the laces of each foot. This activity is great for volleying practice.

TURNING FOCUS

Distance 10-12 yards

☒ Pass the ball against the wall, come toward the ball, look over your shoulder, and turn using either the inside of the foot or the outside of the foot. After turning dribble away and then turn towards the wall and repeat. Alternate right and left feet.

HEADING FOCUS

Distance 1-5 yards from the wall

☒ Practice juggling the ball against the wall only using the head. (no bounces)

☒ Toss the ball high off the wall and then head down to a target to the left or right of the wall. (small goals)

Flicking

⊠ Toss the ball high off the wall and then flick the ball behind you away from the wall.

Clearing

⊠ Toss the ball high off the wall and then with a running start jump off one foot, arch the back and come forward heading the ball high against the wall.

THROW-IN FOCUS

⊠ Throw the ball in from various distances towards the wall. Try to throw the ball so that it contacts the wall low to the ground where a teammate's feet would be. Next, practice throwing to where a teammates head would be. Draw a box as a target. Also practice throwing for distance with a slight run up before the execution of the throw.

WALL GAMES

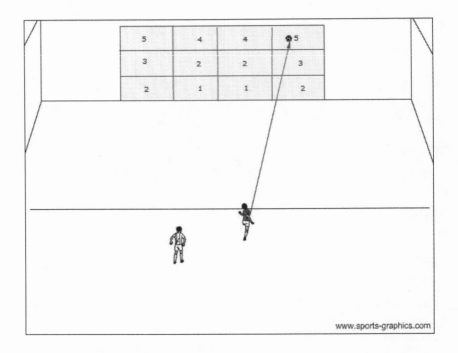

☒ This wall game may be played individually, in partners or small groups. A goal with rectangular boxes (with numbers inside each) are drawn on the wall. Ten shots are taken (behind a specified line) by each player and the total number of points is added together. The player with the most points wins that round.

"Every single day I woke up and committed myself to become a better player." – Mia Hamm (Legendary women's player)

JUST FOR FUN – IMAGINATION

Perhaps the best part of using the wall is in developing imagination and visualization. While playing at the wall, a player can try out new dribbling moves mixed with passing, receiving and shooting. The more time a player spends imagining and visualizing scoring goals while playing at the wall, the more confidence he will have when playing in the real game.

⚽ Maracanã Stadium in Rio de Janeiro, Brazil.

CHAPTER 29

Street Games

"It was against walls and on hard surfaces, whether on the dusty pavements or dry grass, that Di Stéfano discovered his talent dribbling and passing while developing his skills as a sharpshooter with his left and right feet." - Jimmy Burns (La Roja)

In our attempt to create a deeper and broader soccer culture in the United States it is important to teach our players some of the street games that have been played for years in countries such as Brazil. The coach can demonstrate these games at practice sessions to show the players how to play. On the following pages are some games that are played in Brazil. *Information provided by Brazilian coach Carlos Menezes. No doubt variations of these and many other games are played in many countries throughout the world. *Our coaches should challenge the players to be creative and invent a new game that the team can try at practice.

SOCCER TENNIS (NO NETS – STREET STYLE)

www.sports-graphics.com

★ First take chalk and draw a rectangle split in half with a line running through it. The game begins with a service where the ball is lifted (feet) and volleyed to the other side of the grid. The ball may bounce one time after crossing the center line. If the ball bounces twice in the grid after crossing the center line or the opponent kicks it out of play, it is a point for the attacker. If after crossing the center line the ball bounces once and then goes out of play, it is a point for the opponent. When the non-server scores a point they also get service. The ball should be placed and not just kicked with extreme velocity. The first to get to ten points wins.

SHOOT AND CONTROL

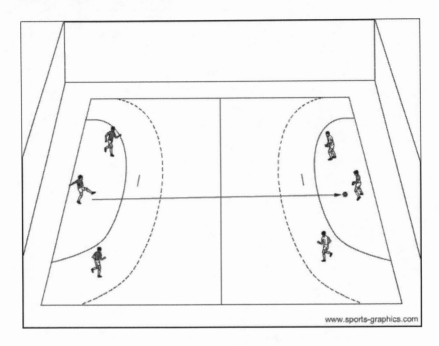

www.sports-graphics.com

★ This game may be played with 1v1, 2v2 or 3v3 on a futsal court or cement area. One player from the attacking team shoots the ball across to the other side of the court. The receiving team must control the ball without using their hands. The ball must be shot below the knees and must pass by the receiving team in order to score a point. The first team to three points wins. <u>Progression:</u> Players may stop the ball with their hands.

IN THE CAN GAME

www.sports-graphics.com

★ In this game each player takes turn serving the ball in the air while the other player tries to score by putting the ball in the garbage can. Handling the ball is not permitted. When playing with single players, a poor service does not count and must be redone. This game may also be played in teams of two where teammates serve to each other. First to three wins the game.

PINBALL

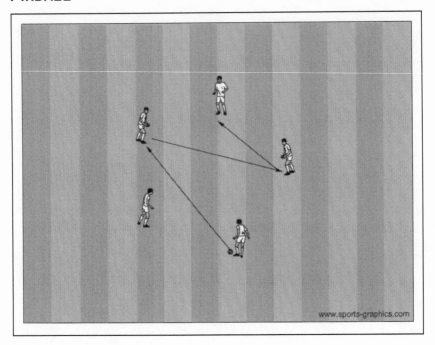

☆ The ideal number for this game is around 4-6 players. This is a passing game that requires an excellent first touch. Players form a circle. The rule is that you must play one-touch, the ball must not leave the ground and it must go directly to the next player's feet. If the ball is lifted off the ground or outside of the receiving player's reach then the player that passed the ball loses a life. The first to lose three lives does a predetermined task.

TIRITOS

★ This game may be played 1v1 or 2v2. Each team takes turns taking 10 shots on goal (shots must be taken from a specified distance – This could be from the penalty spot or from a distance outside the 18 yard box. If there are no field markings then an object may be placed to mark the shooting distance). The team that scores the most goals after taking 10 shots is the winner.

REBOTE

★ This is a 3v3 game where each player shoots from the top of the 18 yard box. If the ball goes in directly it is a goal and shooters rotate. If there is a rebound, one defending player stays in the goal as a keeper and the two other players go out to play a 3v2 game in the 18 yard box. The keeper may only handle the ball within the 6 yard box. Straight rebound = 2 points, a rebound from the crossbar = 3 points, and a rebound from an upper V = 5 points.

CENTROGOL

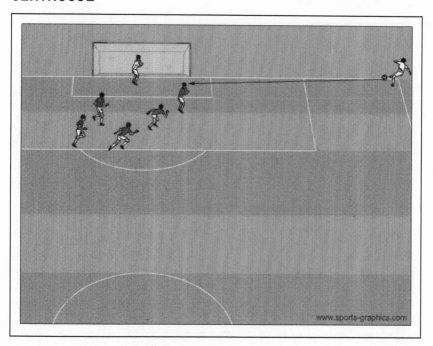

★ In this game there is one goal with a goalkeeper and 3 to 5 attackers. One player takes a corner kick and the other players try to score via a header on the goal. After a player scores, he takes the place of the goalkeeper. The winner is the one who scores the most goals in a predetermined time or who scores a set amount of goals – Example: First to three wins. Variations: A goal may be scored with a volley as well as a header. The person who scores names the goalkeeper.

2v2 PASSING GAME

www.sports-graphics.com

★ In this game there are two teams of 2 players each. The two teams attempt to pass the ball back and forth through a goal. The goal can be made wider or narrower depending on the skill level of the players. The players must play one or two touch and both players must touch the ball before sending it back through the goal. The ball must be played on the ground. A team wins a point when the opposing team makes a mistake. First to ten points wins.

JUGGLE AND SHOOT GAME

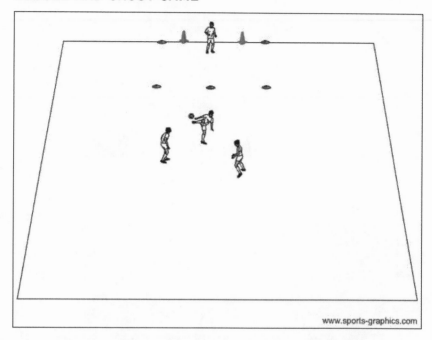

★ Three players juggle the ball and shoot on a goalkeeper from outside a ten yard box. All three must touch the ball before shooting. The ball must be shot on a volley and not touch the ground. If the goalkeeper saves it, he names the next player to go in goal.

CHAPTER 30

Club de Fútbol Atlante:
Youth Development in Mexico

👣 Estadio Olímpico Andrés Quintana Roo – Club de Fútbol Atlante.[34]

During a conference in June of 2012, organized by The

Committee of Galician Coaches in Vigo, Spain, Javier López López[35],

---

[34] Photograph: Wikimedia Commons - GNU Free Documentation License 2009.

[35] Information provided by Atlante Youth Coordinator Javier Lopez Lopez: Galician Coaches Committee Conference Vigo, Spain - June 2012. (www.futbol-tactico.com)

334

Coordinator of the Youth Development Program at Mexican First Division Club Atlante, spoke in detail regarding how elite players are developed in Mexico. He began by explaining that there are various structures that youth development academies may take and that each club fights to establish as many as possible throughout the country.

Structures

1. Centers of High Performance – run directly by the club.

2. Franchises – Someone invests in the center to get it up and running and makes money from the investment. The coaches are given training by the club and the school is given a manual for training where it is outlined how the club wants the youth teams to play. Example: Pachuca has more than 500 of these schools throughout Mexico with approximately 70,000-80,000 players. Atlante has 16 development centers (Centros de Formación)

3. Training Centers in smaller states that are open to all participants.

Incorporating players into the club

Young players arrive at the club in two different ways. Either they come to the school and enroll on their own, or they are brought in through a scouting network. Every six months the club sends scouts

(2-3 coaches from the club) to different states throughout Mexico to find new players. Scouts also work on weekends watching many games throughout the year.

Before bringing players to the club, the scouts search for players with certain characteristics that the club is looking for. After players are brought into the club in preseason, the players are placed in teams according to their age group. After four or five weeks of an observation period, those players who are deemed "good enough" continue with the club while those who are not are sent back to their original clubs. Once this process is complete, the teams begin to train for competition.

Stages of development

The first stage of development at a typical Mexican Youth Academy (called "Fuerzas Básicas") is the stage of initiation (children 5-8 years of age). The second stage is called the stage of improvement (9-12 years of age). The third stage is called the stage of high performance (13-16 years of age), and the fourth stage is called the stage of maximum performance (17-20 years of age).

Stage of Initiation

During this stage the focus is on improvement of motor skills, all technical skills related to the ball, along with basic tactics. What do tactics at this level refer to? Attacking: What the player can do with the ball, pass and move and finish on goal. What the player understands about supporting a teammate by moving into the correct passing angle. Defending: What the player knows about pressuring the ball or marking a player without the ball.

Stage of Improvement

During this stage the main focus is on progressive improvement in the relations of cooperation/opposition of attacking and defending tactics along with continued technical work.

Stage of high performance

Specialization of position within the team begins at this stage. Systems of play are taught along with the important moments of the game such as transitions attack-defense and defense-attack. Tactical situations are taught such as playing a man down, our team is up one goal with five minutes left or playing against a team that high presses etc...

Stage of maximum performance

This stage has the specific goal of preparing the player to play in the first team. Due to the pressure for the first team coach to win, it is very difficult to break into the first team. A player may get a chance to play due to another player's injury or suspension. Another reason for giving a player a chance to play is to show him off for a possible future buyer. Teams in Mexico are not publicly owned, but rather are owned by businessmen who want to recover or improve upon their investment in the club.

Training Methodology and Goals

The primary goal of training at Atlante is to develop players who will ultimately be able to compete at the first team level. Atlante uses tactical periodization based on a model of play to build their training sessions. The model of play is based on the four moments of the game. 1. We have the ball 2. We just lost the ball 3. The opponents have the ball, and 4. We just won the ball back.

Notes: Players are mandated to wear shin guards at all training sessions. In order to replicate the game in training Atlante employs two referees who rotate between the various teams during training sessions. The referees give classes on the laws of the game and their contact with the players gives a human element. In Atlante they have considerably reduced the number of yellow cards due to this concept.

Age Group Progressions of Complexity

Stage of Initiation (ages 5-6): Play 5v5 (1-1-2-1) (ages 7-8) Play 7v7 (1-2-3-1)   Players rotate and play all positions.

Stage of Improvement: (ages 9-10) Play 9v9 (1-3-1-3-1) (ages 11-12) Play 11v11 (1-4-3-3) Players rotate and play all positions.

Stage of high performance: (ages 13-16) Play 11v11 (4-3-3/4-4-2) Players play in specific positions.

Stage of maximum performance: (ages 17-20) Play 11v11 (1-5-3-2/1-3-4-1-2/1-3-4-3) Players play in specific positions adapted to the first team.

Training Sessions and Games (number of minutes)

Stage of Initiation: (5-8) 50 minutes

Stage of Improvement: (9-12) 70 minutes

Stage of High Performance: (13-16) 90 minutes

Stage of Maximum Performance: (17-20) 90 minutes

Note: The time involved in training is the same as a game.

Characteristics of the training session

Training sessions are done mostly in a global (game realistic) manner with ball, teammate(s) and opponent(s) adapted to the model of play. Quality is valued over quantity. Short and intense activities generally adding up to the minutes of active play that mirror the game. (50-60 minutes for a 90 minute game) The number of players may be reduced in order to bring about more repetition of technique, an improvement in perception and more cognitive decisions from the players. Time and space is reduced which helps develop a greater level of intensity and concentration. Activities are done as much as possible with a winner and loser outcome to instill the competitive fire in the players. Placing certain restrictions to achieve the goal of the session is very important. Example: Attacking in wide areas. The players must perform an overlap in a wide area before scoring. Training sessions are built around the Principles of attack and defense. Attack: Penetration, Improvisation, Mobility, Width, Depth. Defense: Delay, Balance, Concentration, and Control.

Basic Structure of a Training Session: High Performance/Maximum Performance

1. A classroom talk about the goals of the session – video, Powerpoint etc…
2. Warm-up = Rondos/Positional Games,
3. Main Part = Coordination and strength circuits, Positional Games, Rectangles, Squares, Game situations, Tactical training, Conditioned Games.
4. Cool Down = Stretching, core strength training

Monday – Session 1: Whole Group (Collective) training (low intensity)
Tuesday - Session 2: Morning - Training by Position (high intensity)
Session 3: Afternoon – By lines and whole group - collective (high intensity)
Wednesday – Session 4: Morning – Specialized training (laws of the game)
etc… Session 5: Afternoon – Simulation of a game competition.
Thursday – Session 6: (Medium intensity)
Friday – Session 7: Shadow Play with low number of opposition 11v2
(low intensity)

Competitions

In the stages of Initiation and Improvement, the competitions are organized locally by Club Atlante, but in the stages of High Performance (13-16) and Maximum Performance (17-20) the competitions are run nationally and organized by (FMF) the Federation of Mexican Football. There are leagues for each year U-13 through U-16. Two tournaments are held each year for the U-13 to U-15age groups where all the teams of the first division come together to play against each other. This includes teams that don't participate in the national league. During the year there are three rounds of play with approximately 45 games per year. Twelve teams from the first division plus four teams from the second division participate. Six teams from the first division don't participate due to distance of travel. In the stage of Maximum Performance there are U-17 and U-20 leagues that parallel the first division. This means that the U-17 and U-20 teams travel together each week and play against same club as the first team. The U-20 team actually competes in the same stadium as the first team.

Note: The number of highly competitive games and the professional training environment that players are involved in within Mexico from U-13 through U-20 has had a direct effect on the success Mexico has had at the U-17 (two time World Cup Champions), U-20 (Third Place Finish World Cup U-20) and U-23 (Olympic Games – Gold Medalist) levels.

CHAPTER 31

Club Atlético Vélez Sarsfield: Youth Development in Argentina

*Information provided by - Guillermo Compton Hall[36]

8 YEAR OLDS:

1ST DAY OF WEEKLY TRAINING

The 8 year olds train two times per week, each practice is divided in three parts of 40 minutes each. The first day of training during the week, which takes place on Mondays, includes analytical technical training with a warm-up of approximately 20 minutes. Technique is also trained another 20 minutes in game-related situations; that is, technical control followed by a pass, a shot on goal, or a change of play etc... The second block of 40 minutes the focus is on possession with a positional game in a 25 by 15 meter grid. This activity is worked in three groups of approximately 13 players per

---

36 Guillermo Compton Hall presently works as a youth coach with Vélez Sarsfield.

group. The coaches continually give different restrictions such as two touch, one touch - if I receive a horizontal pass then I play vertical along with as many other variations as you can imagine. The final 40 minutes is functional training within lines. The groups are separated into three different lines – defensive, midfield, and forwards. Each group works with a separate coach. All work is done with a size 3 ball. The session ends by stretching and an informative talk reminding the players about what was worked on that day. There is always a high level of intensity in training sessions with situations as close to the real game as possible.

2ND DAY OF WEEKLY TRAINING

The first 40 minutes begin with a warm-up with coordination and 3v3 possession with finishing on goal. This training session is on a synthetic surface indoor. During the second 40 minute block, the players work on tactical functional training within a 4-3-1-2 system. The players are shown everything using a ball by means of attacking and defending exercises. This is the way they will be playing over the next six years. This block of time is functional and very didactic. It is slow and methodical where the players are guided towards an understanding of the system of play without any opposition. In the third block of 40 minutes there are 7v7 games despite the youngsters playing Sundays on full fields in the 11v11 format. All the training sessions are with a size 3 or 4 ball while the games on the weekends are with a size 5 ball. We train with size 3 or 4 balls so the youngsters can gain a better control of the ball along with the basic fundamentals.

10-14 YEAR OLDS:

The U10-U14 year olds work under the same methodology called Tactical Periodization. This methodology consists of training all aspects of the game together. (physical, technical, and psychological) All training sessions are directly related to the coach's chosen model of play. Training sessions are run four times per week.

1ST DAY OF WEEKLY TRAINING

The first day after a game which is Tuesday, the players train in moderately reduced space (in order to improve their aerobic capacity), positional games and possession games related to the model of play. The coach's chosen model of play refers to how the team will approach the four moments of soccer, defense, transition from defense to attack, attack and transition from attack to defense. In the second part of the training session there is a focus on attacking with finishing on goal.

2ND DAY OF WEEKLY TRAINING

On the second day of training the players work in tight spaces with few players (in order to work strength for stops, starts, turns) Positional games and games of possession are also used. The second part of the training session is dedicated to tactical functionality based on the model of play.

3RD DAY OF WEEKLY TRAINING

The third day of practice includes more training in reduced space plus exercises focusing on circulation of the ball paying most attention to the proper striking/passing technique of the ball and the speed of the pass. In the second part of training the players work in lines and finish with 30 minutes of regulation soccer.

4TH DAY OF WEEKLY TRAINING

On the fourth day of training, the focus is on set plays, offensive exercises with finishing on goal and play in reduced space with the appearance of the third man. In the second part of the session there is a game of regulation soccer.

CHAPTER 32

Alternate Training Areas and Equipment

In order to create more enjoyable training sessions that are also of high quality, and relative to player development, the coach should begin to gather certain useful training materials. Alternate training sites should also be sought so that players can experience playing on cement, sand etc…

⭐ A sand soccer field in Belo Horizonte, Brazil.[37]

_____

[37] Photograph: Andrevruas – Wikimedia Commons 2009.

✭ Children in Ghana with a ball - ready to play.[38]

---

[38] Photograph: James Hills – Wikimedia Commons 2007.

<u>Balls</u>: futsal, plastic, Brazilian rubber balls, tennis balls etc…

✯ Brazilian rubber balls may be purchased at the following website:

http://www.brasilianfutebol.com

<u>Horca</u> (rope and string on a pole) for heading practice, and <u>hula hoops</u> for use with various warm-up games.

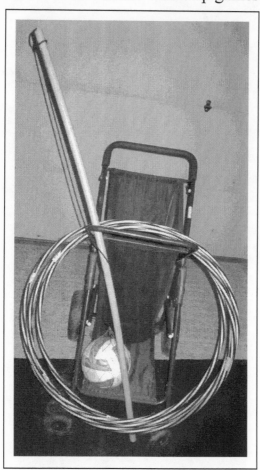

★ Rings and mini cones

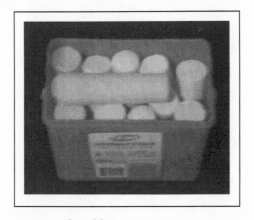

★ Washable sidewalk chalk for marking targets and cement areas.

✫ A great area for individual or team training in Portland, Oregon - USA.

✫ Small squares for a soccer tennis game – Portland, Oregon - USA.

☆ A bucket for a juggling game – Portland, Oregon - USA.

"We try and create other environments so they don't think they have to go to a grass field to play. We take them to play futsal on the basketball court, on concrete. We play soccer tennis on tennis courts. We take them to play on the beach. We try and show the kids, "You can play anywhere." – Cony Konstin (FIFA Futsal Instructor and Director of Coaching at Westside Timbers)

🌏 Children playing in a drained swimming pool in Lima, Peru.[39]

---

[39] Photograph: Enrique Arévalo 2011.

CHAPTER 33

A Place to Play

"I'd create soccer courts all over the place, where children can play soccer or futsal, anytime. You don't need a giant soccer field for that. There are so many abandoned tennis courts they could convert to, multi-purpose futsal courts and let the kids just play." – Cony Konstin (FIFA Futsal Instructor)

★ A futsal goal/basketball hoop combination – Santa Cruz, Bolivia.

Knowing how important it is for our players to play outside of the regular training sessions, it would make sense for us to do as much as we can to create more places for our players to play. I have spent years living in California and Oregon, and in the communities that I have lived, (many soccer first families), children can be found playing soccer in the streets and parks all the time. Balls are continually running in front of cars and I have had to hit the brakes numerous times in order to avoid running over soccer balls.

Of course the children will continue to play in the street or any area they can find, but it makes sense to try to avoid this kind of situation where children can get injured. One idea is to convert tennis courts into multipurpose futsal courts. Goals would not even be required since the children will put down their own objects to form goals. This is certainly an option in urban centers where tennis courts have basically been abandoned due to a lack of interest.

Another idea to increase the number of futsal courts is to alter basketball courts by putting a goal beneath the hoop. This way, children will have the option of playing basketball, futsal or both. In areas where there is rain in the winter, a roof must be constructed to allow for continued use year round. On the following page is an article about a futsal court and structure that is being built by Hacienda CDC in Portland, Oregon. For the same cost as one turf field, around ten of these futsal courts and structures with roofs on them can be built. As a soccer nation, and as a nation that cares about our children, we must look hard at our urban centers and how we can support the children who live there. Of course it makes most sense to put these courts where there are a lot of "soccer first" families and the interest is high, but we should also try to put them in areas where kids are not presently seen playing in the parks.

Soccer court planned to keep Northeast Portland kids out of street

POSTED: Tuesday, February 21, 2012 at 04:31 PM PT Daily Journal of Commerce

BY: Lindsey O'Brien

The neighborhood near the intersection of Killingsworth Street and Cully Boulevard in Northeast Portland is not as dangerous as it once was, according to Luz Maria Gastélum, who has lived in the area for 16 years.

Drug use, violence, crime and prostitution are not nearly as prevalent as they were just a few years ago, she said. But Gastélum, 46, who lives with two young sons, and other families in the largely Latino neighborhood are still concerned about the safety of their children. The lack of outdoor play areas nearby, where approximately 400 children live, creates a different sort of danger.

"We are worried because they play in the parking lot and in the streets, and the kids are focusing on the (soccer) ball and the game, so they're not paying attention to the cars coming and going," Gastélum said via translation.

But the group that owns the three housing complexes near the busy intersection, nonprofit Hacienda CDC, is planning to build a small, semi-enclosed futsal court on the vacant lot near the site. Futsal is an indoor variation of soccer in which five-player teams compete with a smaller, heavier, low-bounce ball on a hard surface about the size of a basketball court.

"I'm scared to death one of the kids playing in the neighborhood will kick a ball into the street and get hurt on Killingsworth," said **Victor Merced**, executive director of Hacienda CDC. "We're serious about building this."

More than 700 people live in the nonprofit's low-income and affordable housing at the Villa de Clara Vista and Villa de Sueños apartment complexes and Clara Vista Townhomes

Villa de Clara Vista, purchased and redeveloped in 1995, is the nonprofit's oldest property. Plans for the futsal court emerged during early discussions about expanding the property's existing community center, which hosts a county health clinic and provides space for community programs including "Vamos Kids," an after-school activity for elementary students, and a gang prevention program called "En Control."

"(The court) would be a good solution and a better place for our kids to play," Gastélum said. The plan is to construct a court measuring 50 feet by 80 feet. It will not have walls, but rather 8-foot-high screens.

★ The Futsal Court at the corner of Killingsworth and Cully Boulevard in Portland, Oregon. (Photograph: provided by Hacienda CDC)

Scott | Edwards Architecture designed the heavy timber-framed structure, which is planned to support an eco-roof to reduce storm water runoff. So far, the firm has contributed its work pro bono, according to principal Sid Scott.

"Right now the balls end up in the parking lot and the street, but this will be a great space that is really designated to kick a ball around," Scott said. "And the structure itself will be visible and inviting to the community."

Hacienda CDC in December raised nearly $6,000 through the Willamette Week's Give! Guide, which the alternative weekly publishes annually to encourage donations to Portland-area nonprofits. The nonprofit also applied for a $60,000 grant through the U.S. Soccer Federation, and other sponsorships may be sought. The entire project is expected to cost a total of $150,000, according to Merced.

"It's not an expensive project, and it's not really complex," he said. "But it is a really important need in the community."

Hacienda CDC plans to submit a request for proposals for the construction project in the coming weeks, and Merced is hoping that ground will be broken in April.

COMPANIES THAT RESURFACE AND RESTORE ABANDONED TENNIS COURTS INTO MULTIPURPOSE COURTS

(*please contact a company in your area if interested in resurfacing or converting abandoned tennis courts to multipurpose courts where futsal could be played.)

www.snapsports.com

(Official Flooring of United States Futsal)

www.flexcourt.com (United States Locations)

www.versacourt.com (United States Locations)

DESIGN FOR THE ECO ROOF STRUCTURE

www.seallp.com/architecture.html

U.S. Soccer Foundation Grants

Field grants are awarded in amounts up to $100,000 and may be used to purchase futsal courts. There is one deadline annually for all grant programs.

U.S. Soccer Foundation
1211 Connecticut Avenue, NW
Suite 500
Washington, DC 20036
202-872-9277
ussoccerfoundation.org

✪ Children in Italy playing in the street.[40]

---

[40] Photograph: Antoine Themistocleous - Wikimedia Commons 2002.

CHAPTER 34

Overcoming Barriers: 4 Worlds United

What is the "fourth world?" When third world people are living in a first world country, there are numerous barriers keeping them from integrating and interacting with the culture around them. Language, literacy, poverty, and other cultural elements can alienate a newcomer, denying them the chance to improve their lives with the advantages provided in the new world around them. This creates a unique living situation where the first and third worlds meet but don't merge, this makes the fourth world. Citizens of the fourth world are often stuck there, unable to activate the resources in their community and unable to return to the third world.

The 4 Worlds United Soccer Alliance effort began with community six years ago. Kerry Greer, a local student and active volunteer, had been working with the Somali Bantu community at Kateri Park in South East Portland, Oregon. She had been involved with the mothers of the community and was helping them with different layers of adjusting to our city, our schools and our culture. Her work with the families led her to the discovery of an important need in every home; the desire for meaningful play. She heard that some of the players really wanted to try to strike out and get onto soccer teams and play ball. The important thing here is that she saw the need and decided to do something about it. Kerry reached out to our local club, South East Soccer Club, and worked through the phone calls, paperwork and other obstacles that make it so difficult to get a 4th world kid onto the field.

A group picture with some of the children at 4 Worlds United Soccer.

The year was 2006, my recreational soccer team was playing at a high level and several of my players were planning to make the move to competitive soccer during the summer. Spring season was on and so was the rain. No practice fields were available and the Development leagues had only just begun so Saturday games were all that we had going. Teams are pretty full in the spring and since there are no practices, match time is at a premium. Bringing new players onto a spring roster is somewhat difficult.

The registrar called me on a Wednesday saying. "We have 3 Somali Bantu boys that really want to play soccer. Mark, you are the only person I know in our club that has studied some Swahili. Think you can find room for them on your team?" The answer was "yes", of course. On Saturday Mohamud and a few of his friends made it onto a field, officially, for their first game.

Mohamud was and is a standout player. It was apparent from his love of the game and the quality of his play that he would thrive at the competitive level. At the end of our recreational season we had a little team picnic and open scrimmage for players and parents and friends. At this event we met Issa Hassan and Mohamed Abdikadir for the first time on field. They were both shockingly good players. By the end of that party I knew that I needed to arrange a spot somewhere on a competitive team for these 3 players. Good fortune and massive generosity from everyone along the way made it happen that summer.

One of the young players from 4 World's United.

That summer the SESC registrar called again. This time it was a bit of a panic. "Can you show up at Powell Park tomorrow to help us out? My son and I are trying to run an open soccer session with the kids at Kateri Park and it's kind of overwhelming! We have the equipment and volunteers will bring the kids down to the field; we just need a coach with some authority to form it up." I arrived on a Tuesday at 5:30PM to find 75 players running around the green space, wildly. The kids were wearing flip flops, hiking boots, and every kind of donated shoe; many were barefoot. SESC had provided pug goals, some cones, bibs, several balls and 2 volunteers to run the session. It was chaos; sweet chaos. I smiled and waded in. It was exquisite. That was six years ago, and we have continued the summer "program" every year since.

Today 4WU runs a session every week for the community. The player count ranges from 30-50 players each time and the event is a very different thing than six years ago. With our care and the support of many volunteers, guest coaches and local community players, the Park Soccer @ Powell event has become a safe environment for children from every part of the world to meet together for a game of casual soccer once a week. It is a place where they can learn some of the rules and traditions of the game and learn to communicate with each other outside of the apartment complex or school. It is a neutral and powerful forum for interaction, learning and growth. It is also a focus point for members of the 1st world community to join in and bring together ideas, resources and energy that slowly but surely folds these 4th world players into the greater Portland community.

During these years many people have connected with and enhanced the lives of these players and their families. Soccer has opened the door to understanding and communication not only with volunteers that work directly with communities like Kateri Park but also for the team families that become involved whenever a 4WU player arrives to a new roster. 4WU players learn about their new home and their new neighbors learn about them and the combined knowledge transforms into something quite impressive.

Soccer provides the opportunity to reach out and help in so many ways and the depth to which people dive in can be inspiring. Individuals have "adopted" players and taken the path and outcomes for several players into their own worlds of care and responsibility. The list of support is too long to recite here but suffice it to say that when a competitive player suddenly needs to have a fee covered for an important tryout or camp, or needs new cleats or a uniform to join in with a new team, or needs a ride to California to try out for the U.S.

Youth National team, the resources somehow surface and keep these players in a system that can be quite exclusive.

For myself as a lifelong athlete and coach for many years, 4 Worlds United Soccer Alliance gives me a tool with which to work around, through, over and beyond our problematic "pay to play" soccer system in the US. Our mission is driven on a very deep level that participation in soccer at the appropriate level for a player, even a great player, is essential to developing a strong and healthy community of citizens from all communities of the world. Soccer allows them to express their value and express themselves in order to come together, here in this place that can be so difficult, different and distant. 4WU has been able to use the power of the sport to bring new and very real possibilities to these players and their families.

MARK VERNA, PRESIDENT OF 4 WORLDS UNITED SOCCER ALLIANCE - PORTLAND, OREGON

The joy of the game.

CHAPTER 35

Thoughts on Player Development in the United States

On the following pages I have gathered thoughts from some prominent soccer people from around the United States as to their thoughts on how to help improve player development and the game in general. They represent club coaches, coaching directors, administrators, columnists and writers all involved in soccer at various levels throughout the United States.

"Let's keep soccer a "player's game."

Juergen Klinsmann - Head coach United States National Team
(Article: Diane Scavuzzo - Soccer Nation, April 22nd 2012.)

Jacob Daniel - Director of Coaching at Georgia State Soccer Association

"We must adopt an open mind and learn from everyone and not fall into an insular mind set of 'this is America and we do things differently here'. We might be in America, but in soccer, we are competing with the rest of the world and can ignore it at our own peril." (Article: The Youth Academies in England's Premiership by Jacob Daniel - 2011)

Paul Gardner - Columnist and writer for Soccer America Magazine

An even worse reaction to the brilliance displayed by Spain - and Brazil is to simply dismiss it as beyond reach. This has been the English attitude for as long as I can remember. Unable - or, more truthfully, unwilling - to match the skill levels, reliance is then placed on tactics and on non-soccer specifics like fitness, and grittiness. This country (the United States) is in an absolutely ideal position to develop a style of soccer based on the Spanish model. We have the talent here, at the youth level, without any shadow of a doubt. Of course we do. And right next door to us, we have a soccer-playing nation that plays the sport in the same way that Spain does: a version based on ball skills. Mexico is not up to Spain's standards ... but it has pulled off some remarkable achievements at the youth level recently, including last year's Under-17 World Cup. That is where all our efforts, all our coaching routines, all our soccer ambitions should be focused. I'll admit that I do not, any longer, see this as a slow process. I think something needs to be done quickly - brutally if necessary - while we have before us this superb example for us to follow, and that we need to make a much stronger effort to learn from the Mexicans. (Article: Spain's brilliant message. Will it be heard in the USA? Soccer Talk with Paul Gardner, July 3rd 2012)

Paul Currie - Coach - San Diego Surf

"The win at all cost mentality must change. The pressure to win at the youth level is damaging. You can be a responsible, hard-working coach who is focused on developing and not win games. Sometimes my teams get "wacked" in a tournament and they can be the better team. In the general flow of the game, their play can be fantastic and the team can still lose the game. If we lose and play horrible, that is different. But often it can happen that teams play well and lose but are clearly developing. Keeping track of winning can hurt the players' development. It is important to develop the players." (Interview: Soccer Nation – SN Staff, September 5th 2011)

Tom Howe - Founder - St. Louis' Scott Gallagher SC. – "I think more
teams need work on the possession game. All the best teams in the world over the years have been great technical teams – like Spain, Barcelona. Teams like that play the best soccer." (Interview: Youth Soccer Insider – Mike Woitalla, March 25th 2011)

Charlie Inverso - U-15 U.S. Boys National Team Goalkeeper Coach
"There is not as much money to be made, but I really believe that once we tap into inner-city talent we will close the gap on the rest of soccer nations who produce better players than us. I would tell anyone who loves the game that coaching in the inner city is the best soccer experience they will ever have. Not only does it give you a good feeling, but once you find that special young player that you see potential in you will be hooked." (Interview: Youth Soccer Insider – Mike Woitalla, May 24th 2012)

Theresa Echtermeyer - National Staff Coach and Instructor for
the NSCAA "I would like to see us all work together more so that we would be supporting our players of all ages and all levels. What I've seen is we really have more opportunities to learn from each other and help each other out, which at the end of the day helps the kids. The more we share ideas and the more we work together the better it is for our kids. So we should always be asking two questions with every decision we make. First, "Is this what's best for the kids?" Second, "Is this what's best for soccer in America?" (Interview: Youth Soccer Insider – Mike Woitalla, April 19th 2011)

Claudio Reyna - United States Youth Technical Director - "One of
the problems (with American youth soccer) is that we have kids bouncing around all over the place, U.S. Soccer youth technical director Claudio Reyna told me last year. Kids frequently switch youth clubs, join travel teams, transfer to other high schools, all in pursuit of better soccer. But, that turnover needs to calm down a little bit. It's better for the development of a kid if they're at one place in the same sort of comfortable environment, rather than move around." (Interview: ESPN – Leander Schaerlaeckens, May 30th 2011)

Karl DeWazien - Coaching Director California-North. "The outcome
of our children is infinitely more important than the outcome of any game they will ever play." (Video: FUNdamentals of Soccer – Karl DeWazien)

Cony Konstin - FIFA Futsal Instructor and Director of Coaching at Westside Timbers Soccer Club. "I'd create "soccer courts" all over the place, where children can play soccer, or futsal, anytime. You don't need a giant soccer field for that. There are so many abandoned tennis courts they could convert to multi-purpose futsal courts and let the kids just play." (Interview: Youth Soccer Insider – Mike Woitalla, Feb 23rd 2011)

John Hackworth - Head coach Philadelphia Union and former U-17 National Team Coach "The emphasis on winning is a detriment to young players because it prevents us from developing technically proficient players, says U.S. U-17 national team coach John Hackworth. And we're not giving them the ability to make decisions. You can't find a youth soccer game where the coaches aren't screaming the whole time, telling kids what they should do and how they should do it." (Interview: Youth Soccer Insider – Mike Woitalla, March 18th 2007)

Jill Ellis - United States Soccer Development Director "It is certainly time for us as a soccer community to acknowledge the coaches who inspire a love of the game, and to truly appreciate the coaches who develop our future national team players. It is time, perhaps, when getting one special player to the next level is recognized as more important than a 19-0 season." (Interview: Youth Soccer Insider – Mike Woitalla, May 18th 2011)

Derek Armstrong - Founder of La Jolla Nomads Soccer Club "There isn't one answer (to developing more special players), because there are so many different things needed to make up that environment. ... It's such a big issue. I think everybody who's anybody in the United States should be involved in that question." (Interview: Youth Soccer Insider – Mike Woitalla, November 22nd 2011)

Phil Wright - Chairman of U.S. Club Soccer – Regarding the new U.S. Soccer Curriculum "Perhaps the most important of the four pillars, given our country's ultra-competitive spirit, is development over winning, especially at the younger ages. For too many years, I have heard coaches and/or Directors of Coaching complain that they will lose players if they focus on development and do not win. In my opinion, this is an excuse for being unable or unwilling to do the necessary education of players and parents." (Article: U.S. Club Soccer – Phil Wright, April 25th 2011)

Ferdie Adoboe - Founder and Director, Ferdie's Soccer Magic

Academy "The conception that my coach teaches me skills and makes me good has stifled the development process in American soccer. Player development in American youth soccer will be expedited when we pass the primary initiative for acquiring skills to the player, thus, involving them in the development process, and equipping them with the knowledge, responsibility, and capability to help each other."(Article: Wordpress.com Player Development : Whose Job is it Anyway? – Ferdie Adoboe, February 24th 2011.

Dr. Tom Fleck - The first Youth Coordinator for United States Soccer

and developer of the National Youth License curriculum. "We must work to create an environment to develop the American player's growth and development! In the past we have tried to train the Dutch way, the Brazilian way, etc. We can and will together create the finest players in the world if we understand the growth, development and specific characteristics of our youth. Distributing the body of information from the "Y" License is the first step." (Article: Youth Soccer in America – How do We Measure Success? U.S. Youth Soccer Coaching Education Department, May 2012)

Tab Ramos - Former United States National Team Player and present

U-20 National Team Coach "We believe the best thing is to have people who are experts at certain age groups. We've been able in less than eight years to identify coaches that we have fit into certain age groups better than others. They teach the game better, and we've kept them in those age groups." (Interview: Youth Soccer Insider – Mike Woitalla, March 26th 2011)

Hugo Perez - Head Coach U.S. Boys U-14 National Team "We want to

make sure that from the U-14s to all the Youth National Teams, they have a very strong base technically, because we feel that technically is where we lack right now in our country," Perez said. "We want to make sure that we put that in the program so that way when (the players) grow up, if they come to the senior national team and they have a different style of play, they always have a good technical foundation." (Article: U.S. Soccer Increased Roles: Development Academy Technical Advisors Enhance Development of Youth National Teams – December 3rd 2011)

Tony Lepore - Head of Scouting for USSF "We're still looking for guys who are good with the ball, who show a comfort level on the ball," Lepore says. "We're looking for technical players first. And at the younger age group we're not going to scratch off the list any guys who aren't getting it done athletically right now. But also we're not ignoring the guys who have something athletically. There's no real formula. The evaluation sheet we have, of course, looks at guys in terms of technique and decision-making, and then athleticism, and we're also trying to get a feel for their mentality. How competitive are these guys? How focused are they? How much impact do they have on a game?" (Article: Soccer America Magazine: Tony Lepore Heads USSF Youth Scouts - Mike Woitalla, December 1st 2008.)

Javier Perez - U-18 Men's National Team Coach "The challenge here is to build up a proper style of play. In other countries, it is smaller and there is a similar type of player. In this country, we have different backgrounds and many different ideas. So bringing players from different teams in different parts of the country and put them together and make them work with the same style of play is the biggest challenge. The way to curtail those obstacles, reach the players early and introduce them to this style without any other preconceived notions." (Article: Can U.S. Youth Catch Mexico? J.R. Eskilson – TopDrawerSoccer.com, August 7th 2012.)

Jimmy Obleda - Director of Coaching at Fullerton Rangers - "We have a curriculum, a booklet. This is what you need to know from 9-10, 11-12, etc. We have had this since 2004. That is why we have been able to do the things we have been able to do for seven years." (Interview: goal.com - J.R. Eskilson, November 11th 2011)

Gary Kleiban – (Coach F.C. Barcelona U.S.A) "We've made good progress in the last 20 years. Yes we have, and we should all be happy for it. However, it's easier going from 40% to 70%, than it is from 70% to 100%. The first jump involves broad strokes. You know, the common sense stuff. The second jump involves the details. You know, where common sense is no longer common." (Blog: 3four3)

BIBLIOGRAPHY

Alcaraz, Álex Sans Torrelles and César Frattarola. (1998). *Fútbol Base Programa de Entrenamiento Para la Etapa de Tecnificación.* Barcelona: Editorial Paidotribo.

Ariel E. Senosiain and Ediciones Corregidor. (2008). *Lo Suficientemente Loco – Una Biografía de Marcelo Bielsa 2da Edicion.* Corregidor: Buenos Aires.

Athenaeum. (1978). *Soccer-Arpad Csanadi Printed in Hungary Third Revised Edition.* Budapest: Printing House,.

Brüggemann, Detlev. (2004). *Fútbol: Entrenamiento para Niños y Jóvenes.* Barcelona: Editorial Paidotribo.

Cezer, M. G. (2006). *El fútbol por dentro: El libro de los técnicos 1^a ed.* Al Arco: Buenos Aires.

Contijoch, F. A. (2005). *"Todo lo que sé de la vida me lo enseñó el fútbol".* Editorial Océano, S.L. GRUPO OCÉANO. : Primera Edición.

Coyle, D. (2009). *The Talent Code: Greatness Isn't Born. It's Grown. Here's How.* New York: Bantam Books New York.

D'Amico, José. (1984). *Fútbol – Consideraciones Sobre Los Fundamentos del Juego.* Argentina: Buenos Aires.

Dweck, C. S. (2006). *Mindset: The new psychology of success.* New York: Random House.

E, Patricia Rieser & Louis. (2002). *Growing Children: A Parent's Guide Fifth Edition.* CA: Underwood Genentech, Inc. San Francisco.

Jamison, Steve and John Wooden. (1997). *Wooden: A Lifetime of Observation and Reflections on and off the Court.* Illinois: Contemporary Books Chicago.

Jean Piaget and Barbel Inhelder. (2000). *The Psychology of the Child.* New York.: Basic Books Inc. New York.

López, J. L. Wanceulen (2009). *1380 Juegos Globales Para el Entrenamiento de la Técnica Editorial .* Deportiva Publidisa.

Mangonnet, V. (2009). *Fútbol Del 1v1 a La Alta Competencia.* mayo de : Serie Educar Juvenilia Ediciones. 1ª Edicion.

Marcelo Gantman and Andrés Burgo . (2005). *Diego Dijo Las Mejores 1,000 Frases de Toda la Carrera del "10" 1ª edición.* Editorial Distal: Buenos Aires.

Oriondo, L. F. (2000). *La Visión de Juego en el Futbolista 2ª edición .* Barcelona: Editorial Paidotribo .

Menotti, Cesar Luis. (1986). *Fútbol Sin Trampa - Editorial.* Argentina: Buenos Aires.

Román, I. (2011). *La Vida Por el Fútbol: Marcelo Bielsa First Edition .* Sudamericana: Buenos Aires.

Ruiz, L. (1998). *"Como Lograr Ser un Gran Futbolista".* Barcelona: Ediciones Deporte y Cultura.

Ruiz, L (2010). *"Fútbol Profesional y Mi Modelo de Juego".* Moreno & Conde S.L. MC Sports.

Ruiz, L. (2001). *Soccer Secrets to Success Things Great Players and Coaches Should Know* Pennsylvania: Reedswain Publishing-Springfield.

Ruiz, L. (2002). *The Spanish Soccer Coaching Bible Volume 1. Youth and Club.* Reedswain Publishing.

Scopelli, A. (1962). *Hola Mister 3ª edición.* Editorial Juventud.

S.L., Moreno & Conde. (2010). *El Modelo de Juego de Barcelona Oscar Cano Moreno.* MC Sports.

Wein, H. (2004). *Developing Game Intelligence in Soccer.* Reedswain Publishing.

Wein, H. (2000). *Fútbol a la Medida del Adolescente.* Sevilla: Centro de Estudios del Desarrollo e Investigacion del Fútbol Andaluz. CEDIFA.

SPONSORS

COMMUNITY DEVELOPMENT CORPORATION

✭ The author with one of the world's great coaches and embassadors of the beautiful game – Cesar Luis Menotti in Buenos Aires, Argentina.